D0196397

ANGEL
····IN MY····
LOCKER

DEVOTIONS
FOR JUNIOR HIGHERS

Independence Public Library

ANGEL
····IN MY····
LOCKER

DEVOTIONS
FOR JUNIOR HIGHERS

MARY LOU CARNEY

Mary Lou Carney (signature)

INDEPENDENCE PUBLIC LIBRARY
175 Monmouth Street
Independence, OR 97351

3991 5670

ZondervanPublishingHouse
Grand Rapids, Michigan

A Division of HarperCollins*Publishers*

For Betty —
Enjoy!

Angel in My Locker
Copyright © 1986, 1992 by Mary Lou Carney

Requests for information should be addressed to:
Zondervan Publishing House
Grand Rapids, Michigan 49530

Library of Congress Cataloging-in-Publication Data

Carney, Mary Lou, 1949–
    [There's an angel in my locker]
    Angel in my locker : devotions for junior highers / Mary Lou Carney.
        p.   cm.
    Previously published as: There's an angel in my locker. c1986.
    Summary: A collection of twenty-five daily devotions, in which a typical
middle school student discusses with his guardian angel problems ranging
from boredom with church to the death of a relative.
    ISBN 0-310-28471-6 (pbk.)
    1. Youth—Prayer-books and devotions—English—Juvenile literature.
[1. Prayer books and devotions.] I. Title.
BV4850.C36   1992
242'.63—dc20   92-3674
                                                                        CIP
                                                                        AC

All Scripture quotations, unless otherwise noted, are taken from the HOLY BIBLE:
NEW INTERNATIONAL VERSION® (North American Edition). Copyright © 1973,
1978, 1984, by the International Bible Society. Used by permission of Zondervan
Publishing House.

"NIV" and "New International Version" are registered in the United States Patent and
Trademark Office by the International Bible Society.

All rights reserved. No part of this publication may be reproduced, stored in a
retrieval system, or transmitted in any form or by any means—electronic,
mechanical, photocopy, recording, or any other—except for brief quotations in
printed reviews, without the prior permission of the publisher.

Edited by Dave Lambert
Interior designed by Dave Lambert
Cover designed by Larry Taylor
Cover and interior illustrations by Matt Mew

Printed in the United States of America

94   95   96 / CH / 14   13   12

With
love
to
Amy Jo,
and
Brett,
who
exasperate
and
inspire
me

This is a book of daily devotions . . .

It may not *look* like a devotional book, and it certainly doesn't *read* like one.

But it is.

We wanted to give you a different kind of devotional book. We thought you'd have more fun with it. And we thought you'd be interested in Andy, too—a middle-school kid just like you with the same problems you have, from being bored with church to getting into trouble with his teachers at school.

So read the prologue on page 8 to meet Herbie and Andy. Then choose a good time during the day to spend with God and read a chapter.

Twenty-five chapters.

Twenty-five days.

You don't have a Herbie in your life—at least not that you can see and talk to. We just made him up.

But we hope Herbie and Andy—two made-up characters—will help you to think about a God who is real. And about how that God can make a difference in the everyday, middle-school problems *you* face.

Prologue

Andy stared into the goldfish bowl. Goldie stared back. "You fish have it made," he said, dropping several flakes of fish food into the murky water. "All you have to do is swim and eat and blow bubbles. Life is just one big pool party for you!"

He walked toward his dresser and looked at himself in the mirror. Freckles. "All the other guys get tans—I get freckles!" He practiced smiling. He practiced not smiling. He practiced waving. He practiced looking tough. "Give it up," he said, throwing himself down on his bottom bunk. "You look like just what you are—a sixth-grader scared stiff!"

He tapped on the side of Goldie's bowl, and she began to swim around and around in circles. Her delicate tail swished through the water. "Dumb fish," Andy said.

"Oh, I wouldn't say that. As a matter of fact, fish are more intelligent than many other creatures God made."

Andy jumped up so quickly he hit his head on the

top bunk. Where had that voice come from? He looked under his bed. Nothing. He tiptoed to his door and flung it open. Nothing. He knelt in front of his closet and peered into piles of cleats and mitts and battered comic books. Nothing.

Andy rubbed his head. "Maybe I imagined it," he said, glancing in the direction of the fish bowl.

He took his comb off the dresser and began working on his hair. First he combed it all back. "No good. I look like a red-headed vampire." Then he combed it all forward. "Now I look like Mom's dust mop." He parted it first on one side, then on the other. He dug the comb straight down the middle of his head and left a crooked trail of scalp showing between two humps of hair.

"Why such a fuss over how to wear your hair? Part it on the left side—that's your best bet. And I think we ought to go to the barber before next Monday."

Andy whirled around and scanned the room. Who said that? He kicked his foot into the pile of dirty clothes. He cautiously pulled out each drawer and poked

at its contents with his comb. He pressed his nose against the window screen and looked left and right.

Then he heard the laughter, soft at first—but growing louder as the seconds passed. It was a little like the tinkling of wind chimes in a breeze, but it had a strange echo about it, and Andy felt a chill run down his spine. He tossed the comb aside and grabbed his baseball bat, turning slowly from side to side, ready to clobber the first thing that moved. "Okay," he said hoarsely, "come on out!"

Suddenly the laughter stopped. "I must say, this is the most *unfriendly* welcome I've had in the last thousand years or so. Put that thing down! You wouldn't really bash your guardian angel his first day on the job!"

Then Andy saw him, curled up in Andy's catcher's mitt. His bare toe was tracing the "Johnny Bench" signature on the glove.

"Who are you?" Andy asked, lowering the baseball bat and taking a step toward the strange creature.

"Herbie's the name. Herbekiah, actually—but there's no need for us to be formal." Herbie stood up. His feet dangled a few inches above the mitt. He floated there, like a helium balloon. He brushed his robe, straightened his halo, and smiled. His teeth were gold—all of them! He fluttered his wings and flew to the top bunk. There he perched on the maple headboard and began reading an open comic book. The pages turned by themselves.

Andy stared. He pinched himself hard to make sure he was awake. Herbie laughed. "Oh, you're awake, kid. And I'm real. Come on over here and relax. I'll fill you in on all the details."

Andy climbed to the top bunk and sat at the foot of the bed. He left both his feet dangling over the edge, just in case he needed to make a quick escape.

"So," Herbie began, "because I'm a guardian angel, I have certain responsibilities. This year I've been assigned to watch over you, to help you through your first year in middle school. I've been taking notes on what middle school is all about."

Herbie pulled a tiny spiral from his sleeve and opened it. "I know about the team sports and the lockers that won't always open. I know about the teachers who take a vow never to smile until *after* Thanksgiving vacation. I know about the problems of making new friends and of deciding where to sit in the cafeteria." He closed the spiral, and it disappeared inside his robe.

"So cheer up, Andy old kid, because God has decided to give you an 'added edge'—me! I'll be around to help you with problems, to show you what's right. Sort of like Jiminy Cricket in Pinocchio—remember?"

Andy managed to nod his head.

"And sometimes—just sometimes—I'll have advice for you. When you've been around as long as we angels have, you're bound to have learned something!" Herbie smiled, his gold teeth glinting in the sunshine.

"Andy," his mother said, stepping into his room, "here's your clean socks and underwear. Make sure you put them *neatly* in the *right* drawers." She glanced at Andy who was still sitting on the very edge of his top bunk bed. "Are you all right? You look a little pale."

"Tell me, Mom—what do you see on my bed?"

"You."

"What else?"

Herbie waved at Andy's mom. He did a backward flip on the pillow and landed with his halo stuck between his wings.

"I see you and a comic book, all right?" Mother replied.

"Sure," Andy smiled. "Me and a comic book."

"Now come down from there and get washed for dinner." she said.

She left the room, and Andy turned to Herbie. "She can't see you?"

"Nope."

"How about my little sister Megan? Will she be able to see you?"

"Of course not!" Herbie said. "Listen, kid, I'm *your* guardian angel. Only *you* can see and hear me."

Andy slid off the bed and walked around the room. "My own guardian angel! Wow! I thought stuff like this only happened in cartoons! This'll be great!" Andy stopped and looked at Herbie. Herbie had floated to the floor and was now practicing his soccer dribble with a Ping-Pong ball. "You sure this whole thing is on the level?"

Herbie flew up to face Andy. "If you can't trust your guardian angel, who *can* you trust?"

It seemed a good enough answer to Andy.

"And now," Herbie said, pulling a small shiny duffle bag from somewhere inside his robe, "where's your bathroom?"

"Bathroom?" Andy asked.

"Yes, bathroom. I want to brush my teeth."

"Brush your teeth?"

"Yes, my teeth!" Herbie smiled his biggest smile, revealing two perfect rows of shiny gold teeth. He tapped his front two and said, "It isn't easy keeping the shine on these babies!"

"Sure. Right," Andy grinned. "The bathroom's right this way."

And together they started down the hall.

* * *

See, I am sending an angel ahead of you to guard you along the way and to bring you to the place I have prepared. Pay attention to him and listen to what he says.

(Exodus 23:20–21)

Angel In My Locker

Day 1

Andy's hand pounded the top of the alarm clock. His fingers fumbled until he found the little switch that stopped its clanging. He opened his eyes. Streaks of sunlight filled his room. He rolled over and leaned his chin on the window sill. It was a beautiful morning! Already the air was sweet with the smell of summer heat.

"What a great day for fishing!" Andy thought.

He was halfway to his tackle box before he spotted the dress clothes hanging on his closet doorknob. Sunday! This was Sunday!

Andy plodded back to bed and lay staring at the ceiling. *God,* he prayed, *it's such a perfect morning for fishing. I know I could hook that fifteen-pounder if I could get to the river early. I just know it!* Andy closed his eyes. He could almost feel the mud squish between his toes as he waded in knee-deep. He could almost hear the "plunk" of his bobber as the huge fish took his bait.

Angel In My Locker

Andy sighed. Soon he would have to get up and get dressed, put on those black dress shoes that hurt his little toe, and go to church. *I don't want to go to church today, God. It's nothing personal against you—honest! It's just that ties choke me and our Sunday-school class is too crowded. And our minister preaches too long. Especially on hot August mornings! Couldn't I worship you just as much along the river bank?*

When Andy glanced again at the window, Herbie was sitting on the sill, fanning himself with his halo. "Morning, kid. Perfect Sunday morning, don't you think?"

Andy got up and took his good clothes off the hanger. He began to button his dress shirt. "Yeah—perfect morning for fishing. I don't see why I've got to get all dressed up like a department-store mannequin and go sit in some stuffy church. Can't I just worship God wherever I am—like down at the river? Is church really such a big deal?"

Herbie flew across the room and seated himself on top of Andy's fishing reel. "Of course you can worship God anywhere! God is a spirit. He isn't limited to one place, like those ugly stone idols some people still worship. And God is in all his creation. It's important for you to know that. But it's just as important for you to know that church *really is* a big deal."

Andy struggled to button the top button on his shirt. How he hated ties! They reminded him of those old westerns where someone was always getting hanged, the big rope noose choking the guy as he swung from a tree limb. Andy thought he knew exactly how the poor victim felt.

Andy shoved his legs into his dress pants. "After Jesus was crucified and resurrected," Herbie went on, "he came back to heaven. He left Peter and the other disciples to form the first church. What a job that was! No buildings, no money. The Roman soldiers even beat up any Christians who tried to meet together. Many of them were killed. But still they kept coming together to worship and pray. And do you know why?"

Andy stopped putting his belt through the loops of his slacks. "No, why? Why would anybody risk his life just to go to *church?*"

"Because," Herbie said, coming closer, "those first Christians knew the importance of church. They knew they needed each other—that ten people worshiping together were a hundred times stronger than ten people scattered out worshiping alone. They knew they became better Christians by coming together to worship and pray."

Andy paused, one sock on, the other still in his hand. "Are you sure that stuff still holds today—that stuff about being better Christians just from worshiping together?"

"Absolutely."

Andy finished brushing his hair and picked up his Bible. *Okay, God,* he prayed, *I'm going to church. Because it's as important as going fishing, even on a perfect August morning. But maybe—just maybe—you could make that big bass sleep late today?*

Andy studied his reflection in the mirror. Smiling, he unbuttoned the collar on his shirt and tossed his tie onto the unmade bed. The fishing could wait till another day—and so could the tie!

* * *

Let us not give up meeting together, as some are in the habit of doing, but let us encourage one another.
(Hebrews 10:25)

Angel In My Locker   17

Day 2

$\mathbb{A}$ndy leaned against the trunk of the big maple tree. He looked up into the evening sky, searching for the first star. He wanted to wish on it. He could remember when he was little and had trouble knowing what to wish for. But that wouldn't be a problem tonight. There were so many wishes he wanted to make!

Got a minute, God? Andy prayed as he watched the first fireflies flicker over the freshly cut grass. *I've got to talk to you about tomorrow. Tomorrow is the day I start middle school. And I'm not sure I want to go.*

Andy remembered when he took a tour of the middle-school building last spring, during Student Orientation Week. The halls had reminded him of the mazes in his *World's Hardest Puzzles* book!

God, what if none of my friends from elementary school are in any of my classes? Suppose my locker won't open and I'm late to homeroom? Suppose I get lost and never find homeroom!

Where do I sit in the cafeteria, God? Is it cool to

sit with a bunch of kids I don't even know? Suppose my schedule gets lost the very first day and I have to just stay in the restroom until time to go home!

And what do I do, God, about those eighth-grade Goliaths? They're just waiting to cream us!

Andy looked up at the sky. Three tiny stars winked back at him. "Missed the first star. Probably just the beginning of a long string of bad luck." He headed for the house and a hot shower.

Afterward, he found Herbie sitting in the middle of the bed, looking at Andy's yearbook from Brummitt Elementary School.

"Looks like last year was a pretty good year for you: fifth-grade president, school chess champ, on the winning relay team for field day."

"Yeah, elementary school was great. The teachers always smiled and never once forgot my birthday. Sometimes, at recesses, I would be the undefeated tetherball champ for weeks at a time. And I really loved those 'smelly stickers' Mrs. Handlon put on my perfect math papers. I wish I was still in fifth grade! Then I wouldn't have to worry about middle school for another whole year!"

Herbie closed the yearbook. "Get your Bible story book. The big one with color pictures."

Soon Andy returned with the book. He and Herbie settled back against the pillows. Herbie opened the book to a picture of a battle. It was mostly done in reds and oranges. Some men were sword fighting. Some were blowing long trumpets. Some were waving their fists in the air and shouting. In the background, huge walls of stone were falling down. And in the very center of the picture was a tall man with big muscles and serious dark eyes.

Herbie pointed to him. "That's Joshua. I remember when he felt just as scared as you do now."

"He doesn't look like he was ever scared in his whole life!" Andy said.

"Oh, but he was. In fact, the two of you have several other things in common. Joshua, too, had to face new territory. But it wasn't middle school he was entering. It was the Promised Land of Canaan. And instead of facing eighth-graders, he faced such gruesome fellows as the Amorites, Hittites, and Jebusites. Like you, he was leaving something he knew for something scary and unknown. And, like you, he told his troubles to God."

Andy stared at the picture. "So how'd it all turn out for him, for Joshua?"

"Great! At the Lord's command, Joshua and his men marched around the fortified city of Jericho. They blew their trumpets and shouted. They watched as the walls tumbled into rubble! Then Joshua took possession of all the land."

"All of it?" Andy asked.

"*All* of it," Herbie replied.

They closed the book and laid it on the bedside table. Andy turned out the light and crawled between his sheets.

Well, God, looks like you did a pretty good job of helping Joshua. A whole country—he captured a whole country! Grandma has this sign on her wall that says GOD NEVER CHANGES. *So could you help me the way you helped Joshua? I don't need to conquer anything—except my own fears. And my promised land is only Westchester Middle School. But I don't think even Joshua could have been any more scared than I am tonight.*

The room was filled with the sound of Andy's clock ticking. Then Herbie spoke, his voice drifting down from the top bunk. "Get a good night's sleep, kid. Tomorrow is a big day for all of us. But you're going to make it just fine. After all, things can't get too bad when you've got a guardian angel in your locker!"

*   *   *

Have I not commanded you? Be strong and courageous. Do not be terrified; do not be discouraged, for the Lord your God will be with you wherever you go.
(Joshua 1:9)

Day 3

$\mathbb{T}$he policeman's uniform was covered with shiny buttons. The handle of his gun stuck out from a black holster fastened to his belt. "Well, I guess that about covers it," he said, standing up and putting on his hat.

Andy tried not to cry. He bit his lip and clenched his fists, but still he could feel the hot tears on his cheeks.

"We'll be in touch as soon as we know anything. Sometimes things like this are never found. Other times we get a lucky break."

Andy watched the squad car drive away. He could feel his parents looking at him. "I'm going in the back yard for a while," he said.

Sitting against the back of the garage and poking at a hole in his tennis shoes, Andy felt the knot of tears choking him again. "It took me six-and-a-half months to save up for that bike, Herbie! Six-and-a-half months of delivering papers through snow drifts and mud puddles. Six-and-a-half months of counting nickels and delivering

Sunday editions. Six-and-a-half months of riding that old Huffy with the rusty fender!"

With the tip of his wing, Herbie wiped a tear from the corner of Andy's eye. "I'm sorry, kid. Real sorry."

"So why'd you let it happen, then? What's the good of having a guardian angel if he's off brushing his teeth every time you need him?" Andy asked angrily.

"Hey," Herbie replied, flying over to where he could look Andy in the eye. "I'm not some lucky rabbit's foot you keep on your key chain. And I'm not some insurance policy that promises you'll never have any trouble. I'm just a special friend to help you celebrate your good times and understand your bad times."

"Well, I sure don't understand this 'bad time.' Some turkey is riding around somewhere on *my* new bike. I've worked and saved like crazy for six months. And now I have nothing—absolutely nothing—to show for it. I'd like to find that guy who stole my bike and bury my fist in his face!" Andy's clenched fist crashed into his open palm, making a wet, smacking sound.

Angel In My Locker   23

"Come on, Andy. Let's jog."

Soon Andy was plodding down the jogging path in the park, his Nikes leaving tiny puffs of dust behind. Herbie was sitting on his shoulder. A small white cloud cushioned Herbie's ride.

"Stealing's been around just about as long as people have," Herbie was saying. "And thieves, unfortunately, are *not* a vanishing species. In ancient times, thieves were killed—whether they stole the king's gold or a loaf of bread to feed their hungry families. But even such harsh punishment didn't stop many people from stealing. And when Christ was crucified, two thieves hung with him."

Andy and Herbie rounded the bend and entered the wooded stretch of the running trail. Wildflowers grew close to the path. The squawk of a blue jay pierced the air. Andy took deep breaths and concentrated on making the ball of his foot touch the ground first, the way his gym teacher had showed him.

"You said you had 'absolutely nothing' to show for all your hard work these past few months. That isn't exactly true," Herbie said.

"Oh yeah?" Andy puffed. "So tell me—what *do* I have?"

"Remember last year when you took that paper route? You weren't sure you could handle it. You were a little scared about delivering all those papers. You didn't know if you had enough discipline to make yourself do it every night, no matter what. And you worried about the responsibility of collecting, of making all the money work out exactly right. But now you know you can do it. What you have, kid, is self-confidence. That's something no one can give you. It's also something no one can steal from you.

"And remember all the compliments you got from

your customers this past year—Katie for never missing the porch, Mr. Winquist for putting his paper between the doors when it's raining? You have the beginnings of a fine reputation. And that's something our thieving friend will probably never have!"

Andy slowed his pace as he entered his back yard. He wiped the sweat from his face with his shirt tail and leaned against the house to catch his breath.

"Okay. Let me get this straight. Some thief gets my Mongoose—and I get self-respect and a good reputation. Right?"

Herbie nodded. "Something like that."

Andy opened the door and started inside. "It isn't fair, you know."

"I never promised *fair*," Herbie smiled.

In the kitchen Andy's mother was just finishing dinner. "Do I have time for a shower, Mom?" Andy asked.

"Sure. But make it a quick one," she said as she slid the biscuits into the oven.

Andy started up the steps. "Hey, Mom. Do you have any of the spray paint left from when you painted the patio furniture?"

"Plenty. It's in the basement. Why?"

"I think after dinner I'll give my old Huffy a paint job," Andy said. "With any luck I can make it last another six-and-a-half months!"

* * *

A good name is more desirable than great riches; to be esteemed is better than silver or gold.

(Proverbs 22:1)

Day 4

ndy tossed his school
books down on the bed. "I'm starving!" he said to Herbie, who stood looking into the fish bowl, making faces
at Goldie. Andy dropped a few flakes of food on top of
the water, and Goldie swam up to eat them. "Even *that*
probably tastes better than the slop they serve at
school!"

Andy picked up the three tennis balls lying beside
his bed and began to practice his juggling. Herbie
crossed his legs Indian style and sat in midair, watching.
"Did you see lunch today, Herbie?" Andy asked.

"Actually," Herbie yawned, "lunch doesn't interest
me. In fact, *food* doesn't interest me."

"Well, today's lunch was even worse than usual.
They served us this rubbery macaroni and this dead
asparagus. Dessert was a piece of mud-colored cake
that practically bent my fork!" Andy kept his eyes on the
balls, trying to keep all three going.

"I hate eating in the school cafeteria! Every Monday
they feed us hot dogs the color of dirty chalk. The rest
of the week goes downhill from there."

Herbie stood up and stretched. "So why don't you take a cold lunch?"

"When Mom packs my lunch it's not much better. She gives me stuff like cheese on whole wheat bread, carrot sticks instead of potato chips, and an apple for dessert.

"Wish I could be like Tom Ferrell. Every day he just eats two Hershey bars for lunch. Two Hershey bars. Every day!"

Andy flopped across his bed and began leafing through his science book, looking at the color pictures of molecules and fossils and polluted lakes.

Herbie sat on the foot of the bed. "What a bother food is! You mortals spend so much of your time either thinking about it or preparing it or consuming it."

"A man's got to eat," Andy said, examining a close-up picture of a Japanese beetle.

Herbie shook his head. "I remember when Elijah said that to God. He was hiding out by the brook Kerith. It was the time that wicked King Ahab and his evil Queen Jezebel were looking for Elijah to kill him."

Angel In My Locker

"I remember that story," Andy said, looking up. "It hadn't rained for years. Everything in the whole country was dry as a desert. The crops wouldn't grow, and the animals were dropping dead all over the place."

"That's right," Herbie continued. "God sent that drought to punish Ahab and Jezebel for all the horrible things they were doing. But they tried to make the whole thing look like Elijah's fault.

"So Elijah took off for the backside of nowhere to hide. He camped beside the brook Kerith and tried to decide what to do.

"Now, the brook was still flowing a trickle of fresh water, so thirst was not the problem. But every few hours Elijah would remind God, 'A man's got to eat.' As if God, who had created the digestive system, needed to be reminded! So God sent him food—every morning and every night."

Andy nodded. "There was a picture of that hanging up in my Sunday-school classroom when I was a little kid. These big black birds had their beaks full of food, and they were dropping it down to Elijah."

"Those were ravens. And twice a day they brought Elijah bread and meat."

"Just bread and meat?"

"Just bread and meat," Herbie smiled. "No potato chips or chocolate bars or grape-jelly sandwiches. And that brook just bubbled plain, pure water—no Coke or root beer or ginger ale."

"Yeah, but things were different then."

"And simpler, too," Herbie said. "No junk foods filled display stands in supermarkets. No pop machines waited on every corner. And bubble gum didn't come in even *one* flavor."

Andy grinned. "Wow, talk about primitive!"

Herbie went on. "Last week in health class you and Lance made a poster—remember?"

"Sure. The Four Basic Food Groups. We showed pictures of foods from the Meat Group, the Bread and Cereals Group, the Milk and Cheese Group, and the Fruit Group. Mr. Laposa stapled it up on the bulletin board in the cafeteria."

"Think about that poster the next time you look at your lunch tray. Believe it or not, a lot of careful planning goes into making school lunches tasty and nutritious."

"*Nutritious,* maybe," Andy smiled. "But since you've never eaten *anything,* how can you say school lunches are tasty?"

"Well—okay, okay, maybe tasty wasn't the right word. I should have said *good* and nutritious. And one more thing—your friend Tom Ferrell and his chocolate bars."

"How can you mention chocolate bars to a starving man?" Andy asked, grabbing his stomach and rolling back and forth on the bed.

Herbie smiled his gold smile. "Don't waste your time wishing you could be like him. Just be glad you have a mother who really cares about you—and about what you eat. I have a hunch Tom Ferrell envies you *that* even more than you envy his Hershey bars!"

"Could be," Andy said as he started down the hall. "But if I don't feed this body soon there'll be nothing left to envy."

"What'd you have in mind?" Herbie asked.

Andy paused on the top step. "I guess a few handfuls of raisins will tide me over until dinner."

"I guess they will at that," Herbie smiled, waving his toothbrush and disappearing into the bathroom.

* * *

Give us today our daily bread.
(Matthew 6:11)

Angel In My Locker

Day 5

The muffled voice of a late-night news reporter filtered up from the TV downstairs. Andy squeezed his eyes shut and began to do his times tables in his head. He did that whenever he couldn't fall asleep, and he hardly ever made it past his 3's. Tonight he was on his 9's before he gave up in disgust.

I just can't go to sleep, God, Andy prayed. *And I know why, too. Tomorrow we get our report cards.*

Really, God, my grades aren't so bad. In fact, they're pretty good. Except for science. Mr. Albert said I would probably get a D—maybe even an F. Last grading period I got a B. My folks are going to kill me, God!

It's because of that stupid leaf collection Mr. Albert assigned. I was going to do it. Honest. But the big game was last week, that book report for Mr. Norris was due, and then Noah spent the night. I was going to hike through the woods and get my leaves last Saturday afternoon, but me and a bunch of my friends played touch football until dark. Then we had

this terrible rainstorm two days before the project was due, and all the leaves fell off the trees in mushy, soggy clumps.

I tried to dry a few in the oven so I'd have something to turn in. But I burned them to a crisp!

When I tried to explain, Mr. Albert just frowned and looked away.

I can imagine what Mom and Dad will say.

And report cards go out tomorrow, God!

Andy crawled out of bed. The floor was cold to his bare feet. He started toward the door.

"What's up, kid?" Herbie asked.

"I'm going to get a drink. Or maybe drown myself."

When Andy came back to the room, Herbie was lying on the window ledge, propped up on one elbow. "Can't sleep?" Herbie asked.

"Stupid question," Andy said. He stuck his cold feet back under the covers. "I'll bet Mom and Dad will think *I'm* stupid when they see my report card tomorrow. A D in science, Herbie! Maybe an F! I should have done that dumb leaf collection for Mr. Albert."

"Yes and no," Herbie said. "Yes, you should have done that leaf collection. But you shouldn't have done it for Mr. Albert. You should have done it for yourself."

"What do you mean?"

"Creation is so *incredible!*" Moonlight streamed through the window and fell on Herbie like a spotlight on an actor. "Human beings have never been able to really comprehend this universe. Sure, they think up their little theories about where all this beauty and order came from.

"But I know the way it *really* happened, kid." In the moonlight Herbie seemed to glow with tiny silver rays. "God spoke the light into being. He willed the dry land to appear. He waved his hand and the earth was filled with plants bearing seed and trees bearing fruit. And *leaves.*" Herbie stopped to make sure Andy was listening. "God smiled, and flowers of every color scattered across the landscape. In his endless wisdom he created root systems and seasons and photosynthesis. God veined each leaf with the wonder of life."

The moon was swallowed by a passing cloud, and for a moment Herbie vanished into the darkness. Then he reappeared, a soft circle of light on the dresser. "Nature is filled with a million wonders, kid."

"I know," Andy said quietly.

"You say that Mr. Albert doesn't understand and that your parents will be mad. Maybe they're all just disappointed that you didn't do the best you could—that you didn't really *try*. Fact is, kid, a *lot* of us feel that way." Herbie's glow dimmed and disappeared.

The room was quiet, a silence as thick as the darkness. Then Andy saw a glimmer of shiny gold, and he knew Herbie was smiling. "Go to sleep now, kid. That leaf collection is ancient history. Sure, your folks are going to be sore about your report card, but they're not going to kill you. A new grading period's started. Mr. Albert isn't the type to hold a grudge, to badger a guy for one mistake. Neither are your parents. Neither am I. And, most important of all, kid—neither is God."

Andy closed his eyes. *I'm sorry, God, if I didn't seem interested in what you'd made. I never really thought about it like that before. But I'll do better. Just you wait and see, God.*

Andy began again to do his times tables, but he didn't even make it to the 2's.

* * *

There is a time for everything, and a season for every activity under heaven.
(Ecclesiastes 3:1)

Day 6

"**I**'m so mad at Mick!" Andy said, kicking an apple core that was lying in the middle of the sidewalk.

"But Mick's your best friend," Herbie said.

"*Was* my best friend. I wish he'd move to Siberia!"

"I've been to Siberia," Herbie shivered. "It is not what you'd call a 'friendly' climate."

Andy scuffed into the park. Three white ducks came quacking out of Spring Hill Lake, hoping for bread crusts. Andy scooped up a handful of pebbles and flung them in the direction of the ducks. "Scram!" The ducks scattered, squawking and flapping their wings. Andy sat down near the bank and tossed pebbles one at a time into the water. "What a creep."

Herbie sat on a dented pop can, dangling his bare feet in the water. "You are, of course, talking about social-studies class today."

"You bet your halo I am," Andy replied. "Mick passed me this folded-up paper. Mrs. Fagen was up front, talking about China and land masses and other boring stuff. So I open the piece of paper real slow. I figure it's a note. But it's a poem of some kind."

"A limerick," Herbie said.

"Whatever," Andy went on.

"There once was a teacher named Fagen
Whose breath could paralyze dragons.
She roamed to and fro.
Her foul breath she did blow
Till they hauled her to jail in a wagon.

But I didn't even laugh out loud, Herbie—and suddenly Mrs. Fagen was there, reading over my shoulder, and I knew I was in big trouble." Andy threw the whole handful of pebbles into the water.

"At least you didn't get sent to the principal's office," Herbie said.

"Big deal!" Andy yelled. "I have to write 'I will learn to respect my teachers and to refrain from writing disgusting limericks' five hundred times! That's seven thousand words, Herbie!" Andy stood up, brushed off the seat of his jeans and started walking toward home. Herbie flew after him.

"But it's not really Mrs. Fagen I'm mad at, Herbie."

"Yeah, I know. It's Mick."

"All the time she was yelling at me, I kept trying to tell her I didn't write that stupid poem. She finally put her hands on her hips and said, 'Well then, young man, just who did?'"

"And Mick just sat there," Herbie said, "coloring in his map of China."

Andy turned into his yard and sat down on the front porch steps. "Mick and the other guys are getting up a late game of bloody-murder dodge ball tonight. But *I* have to write lines. And write. And write." Andy took out his spiral and a pencil and started to write. "You know, Herbie," Andy added, looking up. "I hope somebody smashes Mick real good in dodge ball tonight."

Herbie flew over and sat on the top of Andy's pencil. The point broke with a hard thud.

"Why'd you do that?" Andy demanded.

"It's lousy when friends let you down, kid," Herbie said. "Especially best friends. But it happens. It's been happening for a long, long time." Andy sighed and closed his notebook.

"When Jesus was on the earth as a man, he had friends, too. And from the first time he met Simon Peter, the two of them had a special kind of friendship."

Herbie laughed his wind-chime laugh. "What a character Peter could be! He had this booming voice and the quickest temper I've ever seen. His arms were huge and strong, and his eyes were as dark and restless as the Sea of Galilee. But he was *smart,* too. Peter was the first among the disciples to realize that Jesus was really the Messiah, the Son of God."

"Sounds like the kind of best friend I'm going to look for," Andy said. "Someone who's strong and smart. Mick wasn't much of either."

"Anyway," Herbie continued, "the night Judas betrayed Jesus, Jesus warned his disciples that they would all run out on him, that every one of them would desert him. Peter got so mad! He crashed his big fist down on the table and shouted, 'Not me, Lord! Maybe everybody else here—but not me. I'd die before I'd desert you!'"

"Not like Mick *at all*," Andy said.

Herbie looked at Andy. "But before the night was over, Peter denied even *knowing* Christ. Not once, but *three* times. And yet he was Jesus' friend." Herbie paused. "Why do you suppose Mick didn't own up to writing that poem?"

Andy shrugged his shoulders. "I don't know. Chicken, I guess."

Herbie nodded. "Mick's silence, just like Peter's denials, was caused by fear. When Peter realized what he had done, he actually went out and cried—hard! He was so ashamed, so sorry." Herbie was silent for a moment. "Bet Mick isn't feeling too great right about now, either."

Andy was silent.

"Being friends is more than sleeping over or riding bikes or sharing secrets. It's accepting each other—good points, bad points, shortcomings. It's being able to make a stupid mistake once in a while without being exiled to Siberia."

Andy poked his broken pencil point through the holes in his spiral. "Guess I've been known to do a few stupid things myself," Andy said. Then, with a sigh, he stood up and started inside.

"What are you going to do, kid?" Herbie asked.

"Well," Andy replied, holding the screen door open so Herbie could fly in, "I'm going to write my lines and do my math. Then I'm going to call Mick and check my math answers with his. But first," Andy smiled, "I'm going to go sharpen this pencil."

*　*　*

Do not judge, and you will not be judged. Do not condemn, and you will not be condemned. Forgive, and you will be forgiven.

(Luke 6:37)

Day 7

I *have my first piano recital next Sunday, God. And I don't think I can do it.* Andy opened his eyes and stared hard at the piece of music opened on his piano. The tiny black notes stared back. He arched his fingers over the keys and began to play. But a sour chord stopped him cold.

You see, God! Every time I try to practice, my fingers just seem to trip over each other. Tomorrow is my last lesson before the recital. Mrs. Jones will expect every note to be perfect, God!

Every time I go for a lesson she sits beside me on the bench, her back so straight it looks like she has a board in it. She has a moustache of these little black hairs that wiggles when she pooches up her mouth to count. I sweat through my whole lesson— every week!

And now, God, I've got this crazy recital!

Andy went back to the beginning of his piece and started again. But he lost his place when Herbie appeared out of nowhere and landed on a B-flat with a dissonant plunk.

"So, kid," Herbie said, smiling his brightest smile, "only a few more days before you are ushered into the world of professional music. Today Mrs. Jones's living room—tomorrow Carnegie Hall! I can see it now." Herbie moved his arm across the imaginary words. "Introducing Andy the Awesome and His Incredible Keyboard Feats!"

"Not funny," Andy said. "After this recital I'll probably be known as 'Andy the Awful.'" He managed a small smirk. "Besides, I play with my hands—not my feets."

"Maybe, but it sounds like a classic case of cold feet to me," Herbie said.

"More like a case of ten thumbs." Andy got up and went to the kitchen for a glass of cold milk. Herbie followed.

"You're really uptight about this, aren't you?"

Andy sipped his milk slowly. "It's just that everybody's making such a big deal about this recital. Mom's so excited. She's even invited Aunt Libby and Uncle Denny to drive over from Richmond and hear me. She's

Angel In My Locker   39

baking my favorite double-chocolate layer cake to serve afterward.

"I'd like to make everybody proud of me—including myself. And I know all the notes in the recital piece. But when I think of all those people—staring at me, waiting for me to make a mistake—my fingers turn to stone!"

Andy went back to the piano and sat down at the keyboard. He began to play his scales with an ease born of repetition.

Herbie listened for awhile. "Remember in second grade, when you were in the Thanksgiving play at school?"

"Sure," Andy replied without missing a note. "I had to wear this huge headdress with paper feathers on it and play the part of Massasoit. I remember Mrs. Hammond took her lipstick and put a few swipes on my cheeks to make me look more like an Indian."

"You cried yourself to sleep the night before the performance. That morning you begged your mother not to come and see the play. But she *did* come, and you did a *fine* job."

"Yeah, but that isn't exactly in the same league with this piano recital stuff."

"Yes it is, kid. You see, you thought that audience back then was waiting for you to fail, to make a fool of yourself. But of course they weren't. And the audience next Sunday won't be, either. People who love you will be in that audience, people who are already proud of you. People like your family and your piano teacher." Herbie tipped his halo and bowed. "Even your guardian angel will be there."

His halo back in place, Herbie continued. "You've already asked God for his help, and he always gives it. But he won't do for you the things he wants you to do for yourself. So get back to practicing. And watch your rhythm!"

Andy finally played the piece through twice without any mistakes. Herbie applauded. "What'd I tell you? You're going to be great at the recital!" He flew down to the keyboard and said, "Hey, kid. How about a duet?"

"Sure! What do you know?"

"Only everything," Herbie grinned.

And soon a rather jazzy version of "Heart and Soul" could be heard coming from Andy's living room.

* * *

I can do everything through him who gives me strength.
(Philippians 4:13)

Independence Public Library

Day 8

Andy rolled over and snuggled deeper into his covers. Outside the wind whistled and moaned as it raced around the corners of the house. Andy opened his eyes and looked at the clock. Eight o'clock!

"Oh, no!" Andy groaned. "My alarm didn't go off!" But as soon as his feet hit the cold floor, Andy remembered. There was no school today! School was cancelled because of the blowing and drifting snow.

Andy threw on his dirty socks and went to look out the window. Snow was everywhere! It lay in fluffy whipped-cream drifts, covering shrubs and walks and even roads.

"Herbie! Herbie!" Andy yelled. "It snowed last night! Boy, did it snow last night! Come and see. It looks like a giant Christmas card, the kind Aunt Rachel sends with all the bumpy glitter."

Herbie appeared beside Andy and looked out the window. "Snow! No matter how dingy or dirty things may look, a good snowfall wraps everything in sparkly white." Herbie smiled. His gold teeth shined especially bright today. "And white *is* my favorite color."

"Everything really does look neat—so different from yesterday," Andy said. "It's all so fresh and unspoiled. This must be how the whole world looked before man messed it up with pollution and junk."

"Just about," Herbie said.

Andy jumped off the bed and began rummaging through his drawers for his long underwear. "I have to get outside and shovel some sidewalks. Mr. Hooper paid me four bucks last year for shoveling his."

Herbie was still sitting on the window sill, looking into the brightness of the backyard. "I guess that's the thing I like best about snow—the way it changes something ugly into something beautiful."

Andy pulled out a pair of heavy wool socks and put them on over his dirty ones. "I bet some of those drifts are waist high. Maybe higher!"

Herbie glanced toward Andy, who was busy piling on layers of clothes. "You know, kid, God can change human nature, too."

Angel In My Locker   43

"What'd you say?" Andy asked, pulling his ski mask and wool scarf off the top shelf of his closet.

"I said," Herbie replied, standing up and raising his voice, "that God can change people just like he can change the scenery. Actually, the Old Testament prophet Isaiah says it best. He compares God's forgiveness to snow. 'Though your sins are like scarlet, they shall be white as snow.' "

"We have this girl in our school named Scarlet."

"I'm talking about the color scarlet—you know, red!"

Andy looked at Herbie. "As soon as I finish shoveling walks, I'll see if some of the guys want to build forts and have snowball fights."

Herbie sighed. "Listen, kid. The point I'm trying to make is that God has the power not only to cleanse the landscape, but to cleanse human hearts as well."

"Sure, Herbie. And then later I might help my little sister build a snowman." Andy started down to the hall closet, where he kept his boots and heavy coat.

Herbie shrugged his shoulders and said, "Human beings! Now I know that a snowday from school is not the best time to explain the plan of redemption."

Herbie flew downstairs and found Andy pulling on his last mitten. Herbie knew that under his ski mask Andy was smiling. Herbie smiled, too.

"Come on, kid. The theology lesson can wait."

"Theology lesson?" Andy asked.

"Some other time," Herbie said, snuggling down into the hood of Andy's sweatshirt. "Now let's go make a few snow angels!"

* * *

**He says to the snow, 'Fall on the earth,'
. . . so that all men he has made may
know his work.**

(Job 37:6–7)

Angel In My Locker

Day 9

Andy knelt beside his bed. He folded his hands and leaned his head forward until his forehead was resting on his thumbs. When he was little, every bedtime prayer was said in this exact position. But tonight's prayer was much harder to pray than those "Now I lay me down to sleep" ones.

I've got a problem, God, Andy began. *A really big one.*

We're having this big grammar test next Friday. Mrs. Miles has covered the board with diagrammed sentences, assigned a zillion practice exercises, and even played "Grammar Bingo" with us—but Dave somehow can't seem to understand the parts of speech. He says they all just look like words to him.

And so he asked me to help him cheat on the test.

He sits right behind me. All I have to do is write big and not cover up my answers.

All the guys say they'd be glad to do it—but the other smart guys don't sit close enough to Dave, and the rest wouldn't be much help.

And we won't get caught. No one will ever know.
Besides, God—I don't want to let Dave, and every-body else, down.

Andy got up off his knees and sat on the side of the bed. He picked up his Bible and began to read in John.

"Try chapter fourteen, verse one," Herbie said as he fluttered down and sat on top of Andy's alarm clock.

Andy turned to the scripture. " 'Do not let your hearts be troubled. Trust in God; trust in me.' " Andy read. "Well, Herbie—*my* heart is *plenty* troubled!"

"Yeah, I know, kid."

"What am I going to do? Doesn't the Bible say we're supposed to help each other?"

"Acts twenty thirty-five," Herbie said.

"And how about being kind to each other?"

"Ephesians four thirty-two—and lots of other places."

"I knew it!" Andy said. "And that's all I'm doing—really. Just helping Dave."

"You think Dave's biggest problem is his school work?"

Andy shrugged. "Isn't it?"

"Nope."

"What, then?"

"Dave's biggest problem is that he is determined to do something dishonest—cheat. And he wants you to be part of that scheme. The two of you together will lie to Mrs. Miles."

"Wait a minute—nobody said anything about lying."

"But that's what you'll be doing, kid. You and Dave are going to tell her—through his test scores—that Dave understands the parts of speech, that he is ready to move ahead in his studies."

Andy was quiet for a moment and then said, "All I want to do is *help* Dave. There's nothing wrong with that, is there?"

"You keep saying the only reason you're going to cheat is because you're such a great guy, because you want to help Dave. Are you sure that's the real reason?" Herbie asked.

"What else?"

"You just might want to play the hero, to have Dave tell all the other guys what a great pal you are."

While Andy tried to think up an answer, Herbie added quietly, "Or you just might be afraid—of what Dave and the others will think of you if you don't.

"And what kind of help is cheating, really? Dave won't know any more about grammar. He won't be any less confused by copying your answers. It will only teach him to be dependent—and to be dishonest. Seems to me, if you're really his friend, you could teach him more than that!"

"You make the choice sound simple—but it's not!" Andy said.

"I know it's not, kid," Herbie said softly. "But nothing good ever comes from dishonesty. That churning inside you is your conscience—sort of a built-in radar system to steer you away from sin. And cheating *is* sin. You say no one will ever know. But you'll know and I'll know. And God will know, too."

"So what am I supposed to do, Herbie? Stay home sick the day of the test? Change schools? Join the Marines?"

"You asked God what to do. Now you're asking me what to do. Listen to your heart—and your conscience. You already know what to do."

Andy walked across the room and flipped off the lights. He made his way through the darkness and climbed into bed. "Dave won't be too happy if I let him flunk that grammar test."

"Just tell him you don't cheat—and you like him too much to see him lie his way through school instead of getting the education he needs. Besides, there's still a few days left before the test. Why not try a little tutoring, just the two of you?" Herbie asked.

"Dave's got an awful lot to learn about prepositions and adverbs and nouns," Andy said.

"He's got a lot to learn about honesty, too," Herbie added. "And maybe you can teach him."

"Maybe," Andy sighed. "Maybe so."

*   *   *

We have renounced secret and shameful ways; we do not use deception.
(2 Corinthians 4:2)

Angel In My Locker

Day 10

The only sound in the room was the hissing of the vaporizer. It had been sputtering out steam night and day all week long. Never once had Andy's mother let it run dry. Andy closed his eyes and listened. The bubbles and gurgles sounded like spaghetti sauce simmering.

For six days Andy had had to stay in bed. He was only allowed up to go to the bathroom. Ever since the doctor told his mother that Andy had pneumonia, she had made him lie perfectly still. The first few days Andy was afraid he was dying from the pneumonia; now he was sure he was dying from boredom.

Oh, God, Andy prayed. *I want to be well again! I'm tired of cough syrup and pills and blankets. I'm tired of hot soup and thermometers. I'm even tired of 7-Up!*

Herbie was relaxing on top of a stack of tissues. "So how's it going, kid?"

"About like it looks," Andy grumbled. "I'm being held hostage in my room by a germ the size of a pinhead. And I am *bored.*"

Herbie shoved a fresh straw into the glass of 7-Up. "How about something to drink?"

"Ugh! Give me a break! All I do is drink that stuff all day long."

"Well, you know what the doctor said. He said that fluids are *the* most important thing you need. Remember—there's a war going on inside your body!"

Andy coughed, a deep, full cough that tore at his insides. "The way my chest feels, it must be on the losing side for sure!"

"Let's see what your mom left for you to do," Herbie said as he began to plow through the stacks of stuff on Andy's bedside table.

"Spare me the inventory," Andy said. "I already know it by heart. There's eight comic books I've already read a million times, a bunch of old *Good Housekeeping* magazines, a deck of UNO cards, and my little sister's *Jumbo Activity Book*."

Herbie looked at the clutter of magazines and books. "You say you're bored, kid. Well—that's a good

Angel In My Locker   *51*

sign. It means you're getting better. So how'd you like to get to know some of my friends?"

"I don't think I'm quite ready for an angel choir, if that's what you have in mind."

"No, no! Nothing like that," Herbie grinned. "I just thought you might want to meet some really interesting people—heroes, even."

"Why not?" Andy shrugged.

"If you'll dig deep, under the comics, you'll find your mother also left you a Bible."

I'm being held hostage in my room.

Andy reached under the stack of comics and cards. Sure enough, his Bible was there. He pulled it out and placed it on top of the covers beside him.

"Your doctor is right, you know, when he says there's a war going on inside you," Herbie said.

"I know, I know," Andy choked out between coughs. "My body is fighting to get rid of invaders."

"In Bible times," Herbie began, "battles were a common thing." He flipped open the Bible to the book of Joshua. "Remember just before school started, when I told you about Joshua and the battle of Jericho?"

Andy nodded.

Herbie turned a few pages. "Here in Joshua ten it tells about a battle where even the *sun* took sides." Herbie shoved an UNO card in to mark the place. "And in first Samuel seventeen you can read about that big bully Goliath and David the hero." He turned to the passage and used another card for a bookmark. "You know, kid, David was just about your age when he met that monster of a Philistine."

"I'm glad the Goliaths I worry about in middle school are mostly in my head," Andy said.

"Read Exodus fourteen," Herbie said, leafing toward the front of the Bible. "It tells all about what happened to the evil Pharaoh, his fancy chariots, and all his fine war horses."

"Okay, okay!" Andy laughed. "Enough already. Scoot that glass of 7-Up my direction and let me read."

Later, when Andy closed his Bible, he looked up at Herbie. "Wow, that was something! I could see the whole thing in my head. Those stories would make great comic books!"

"Guess they would at that," Herbie said. "Each of those battles was so important to God that he became personally involved in it. And your battle with pneumonia is just as important to him."

"Good," said Andy as he leaned further into his stack of pillows and closed his eyes, "because I need all the help I can get."

"Just you rest, kid," Herbie said, pushing the Bible to the far side of the bed. "And don't worry."

A sleepy grin tugged at the corners of Andy's mouth. "Better look out, you germ invaders," he said. "God's got the joy stick for this one—and his record is hard to beat!"

* * *

Where does my help come from? My help comes from the Lord, Maker of heaven and earth.

(Psalm 121:1–2)

Day 11

Andy stood in front of the dresser mirror, towel-drying his hair. He leaned in close and stared at his face. He checked for the first sign of a beard, but his cheek was almost too smooth. "What you need," Andy said to his reflection, "is a couple of good scars—or at least a broken nose. Then you wouldn't look like such a wimp!"

Andy stretched out on the floor and began doing push-ups. Then he did sit-ups. He ran in place for five minutes. Finally he fell on the bed, his heart pounding in his ears. When the beating sounds grew softer, Andy rolled over on his stomach and watched the sky fill up with stars. The weight inside him refused to shift. He knew what he had to do.

Well, God, Andy began. *I've got to tell you something. I don't really want to tell you, but I know I have to. I stole a candy bar today. From old Mr. Whilton's store.*

See—Juan told this stupid dirty joke in the locker room after PE, and I didn't get it. So I didn't laugh with all the others.

After school Juan kept calling me "wimp" and "sissy" and "baby." He kept ribbing me about how "innocent" I am.

Then, at Mr. Whilton's, he dared me to take a candy bar. He said it would take a "real man" to swipe something with Mr. Whilton standing right there. So I stole a Snickers. I stuffed it inside my jacket and Mr. Whilton never knew. We all shared the candy on the way home, but my piece tasted like lumpy rubber.

And now I don't feel macho or big. I just feel mean and rotten.

Andy walked back to the dresser and began combing his damp hair. Herbie hovered to one side of the mirror, watching. Andy slicked his hair straight back and gave himself a mean stare. He tried to lower his jaw and look tough.

"Don't tell me," Herbie said. "You're practicing for the Bulldog Imitation Pageant."

"Very funny," Andy said, sinking onto the bed. "My whole life may be coming apart and you make jokes."

Angel In My Locker

"Sorry, kid. It's just that you look so funny when you make those faces!"

"I'm not trying to be funny—I'm trying to be manly!" Andy yelled. "How do I know there's nothing wrong with me? Maybe I'm not normal. I don't seem to fit in with Juan and the guys anymore. And when I *do* do something to prove I'm a real man—like tell a dirty joke or steal that candy from old Mr. Whilton today—I feel worse than ever."

Herbie settled on the bed near Andy. "You and your friends have a rather one-sided idea of what a 'real man' is."

I stole a candy bar today.

"What other side is there?" Andy asked.

"Why don't you ask the bravest, smartest, most masculine man who ever walked the earth?"

"Samson?" Andy asked.

"No," Herbie replied. "Jesus.

"He was raised to be a carpenter, like Joseph. Long hours of hard work calloused his hands and enlarged his biceps. But that didn't make him a man.

"Then he began traveling from village to village, preaching God's message of repentance. Soon he was confronted by strong enemies—who tried to trick him, embarrass him, even kill him. Yet Jesus never stooped to cheap shots. He did what was *right,* not what was *popular.*

"He took time for children and old people, for the sick and the poor. He really *cared* about other people.

"He liked to look at stars and trees and wild lilies. He never pretended to be something he wasn't. And he even cried."

"Jesus actually cried, after he was all grown up and everything?" Andy asked.

"More than once," Herbie replied. "Because being a 'real man' doesn't mean you have to be tough and rude and selfish. Being a 'real man' means, in fact, just the opposite. It means caring for the problems and feelings of others. It means having a gentle strength that lets you stand up for what is right. It means facing your problems head-on and not blaming others for your mistakes."

"You mean laughing at dirty jokes and swiping candy bars and talking tough won't make me a man?" Andy asked.

"Not even if you live as long as I have," Herbie confided. "And I'll let you in on a well-kept secret. The guy who acts the toughest is usually the one most worried about whether he's a 'real man.' Because a real man never feels he has to prove his manhood to anyone except himself."

Andy was quiet for a while, and when he finally did speak, there was a new confidence in his voice. "I guess this afternoon was pretty dumb. There's nothing manly about stealing. And there's nothing manly about letting yourself be talked into doing something stupid just to prove how 'macho' you are."

"You know what a 'real man' would do in this situation?" Herbie asked.

Andy sighed. "I'm afraid so. Looks like I've got to ask both God *and* Mr. Whilton to forgive me."

"It won't be easy, kid," Herbie said. "But sometimes being a man is a tough, tough job."

* * *

Blessed is the man who makes the Lord his trust.

(Psalm 40:4)

Day 12

"**W**here did all this junk come from?" Andy said, his voice muffled as he crawled even deeper into the closet. He tossed out rusty batteries and pieces of race track and baseballs with the sides hanging loose like tongues.

"Well, kid," Herbie said, dodging a glow-in-the-dark Frisbee that Andy pitched aside, "since it's *your* closet, I suppose you put it all in there."

"I'll need a *truck* to get rid of all this garbage! Mom said she wanted it 'deep-down spanking clean. And she stressed the word 'spanking.' "

Andy sorted the stuff into three piles as he went through it. One pile was for his baby sister, Megan. Another was to give to his little cousin Nathan. The last pile was to be stuffed into garbage bags and put out for the trash men in the morning.

It was the middle of the afternoon when Andy found it—on the floor in the very back corner, buried under boxing gloves and Dr. Seuss books: his collection of Matchbox cars.

Angel In My Locker

"Wow!" Andy said, unsnapping the lid on the big blue case. "I forgot about these." Shiny cars of every color stood in little plastic partitions. "Boy, did I love these things! Scott and I used to race them on the kitchen linoleum." Andy revved the wheels across his open palm. "And we'd have deliberate head-on collisions on the front sidewalk. This '57 Chevy survived hundreds of smash-ups." Andy proudly held up the tiny fin-tailed car.

"You sure have enough of them," Herbie said.

"Ninety-two," Andy said as he replaced the Chevy and ran his finger across the tops of the cars. "Every Saturday morning when I got my allowance I'd race to the dime store for a Matchbox." Andy picked up a sleek yellow car. "This was my favorite—a '62 Corvette. I used to pretend it was real and I was actually driving." Andy put the car back in its space and snapped the case shut. He leaned against the closet door. "My only worries then were whether the dime store would have the car I wanted—and whether Scott would collect more models than me." Andy pushed at the cases with his toe. "Things are so complicated now."

Herbie sat on the top case and let his legs dangle over the side. "Growing up is a little scary, huh, kid?"

"Sometimes," Andy said, placing the Dr. Seuss books in Megan's pile.

"Remember when you were trying to teach your baby sister to walk?" Herbie asked.

"Sure," Andy smiled. "Her grip on my finger practically cut off the circulation!"

"Megan was scared to take that first step," Herbie said. "She was so afraid of falling."

"Oh, she fell down lots of times! But every time she fell I picked her up and set her on her feet again. Then one day she stood alone for a few seconds. I'll never forget that surprised look on her face when she realized nothing was holding her up," Andy laughed.

"With lots of encouragement from you, she managed to put one foot in front of the other—and she was walking."

"Yeah," Andy said. "And then in no time at all she was running all over the house."

"That's where you are now," Herbie said. "Taking those first steps toward being an adult. And it's scary."

"Sometimes I feel like I'm playing a new game, and somebody keeps changing the rules without telling me."

"But some things never change, kid—like God's love for you. He's there to help you through the changes in your life, to believe in you so you can believe in yourself."

"And what happens when *I* fall down, the way Megan kept doing?" Andy asked.

"When that happens, God is right beside you to pick you up. So hang in there, kid. You'll be running before you know it."

"I sure hope so." Andy picked up the Matchbox cases and stood staring at the three piles on the floor. Then he turned to Herbie. "I think I know just the place for these."

Standing on his desk chair, Andy put the collection of cars on the top shelf of his closet. "For old times' sake," he grinned at Herbie, who was swinging Tarzan-style from the closet light chain.

"Why not, kid!" Herbie said, clicking the light off in Andy's spanking-clean closet.

* * *

When I was a child, I talked like a child, I thought like a child, I reasoned like a child. When I became a man, I put childish ways behind me.

(1 Corinthians 13:11)

Angel In My Locker

Day 13

$\triangle$ndy spun the center knob of his lock. Then he began his combination: 12 right, 36 left, 3 right. Click. Andy smiled as he opened the door, remembering how—at the beginning of the year—he had worried about getting his locker open, about remembering his combination.

Herbie was sitting on the top shelf. "Well, if it isn't my favorite human being!" He flew out and perched on top of the door. "That student-council meeting sure lasted long enough."

"It takes a while to plan a party as special as this one is going to be," Andy replied, tossing his *Adventures In Literature* book out onto the floor. The sound echoed in the empty hallway. "The decorating committee is making these giant crepe-paper flowers to hang from the ceiling. We're having the disc jockey from the high-school radio station take care of the music. He has *all* the best records! And there'll be gobs of food: chips and cake and mints and punch." Andy picked up the armload of homework and looked at Herbie. "There's just one problem."

"Only *one?*" Herbie teased, flying off the door just before Andy banged it shut.

"Some of the guys are going to take dates. And, well ... there's this girl I'd like to ask."

"I'll bet it's Katrina."

Andy smiled. He could feel his cheeks redden with just the mention of her name. "Isn't she pretty, Herbie? She's just about the prettiest girl in the whole school!" Andy and Herbie started toward the door. "When she smiles," Andy went on, "she has two huge, perfect dimples. And she hardly ever giggles or acts silly like the other girls in our class." Then he frowned. "But she's tall. Taller than me. Lots taller."

"Is that the 'one problem'?"

"No, not really," Andy said, pushing open the door. He walked over to his bike and strapped the books on behind his seat.

"So what *is* the problem, kid?" Herbie prodded. "The suspense is killing me."

"I'm afraid she'll turn me down." Andy unchained

Angel In My Locker

his bike and straddled its black leather seat. Herbie settled into the crook of the handlebars. "She's plenty friendly to me at school, but—let's face it, Herbie. I'm incredibly ordinary."

"Ordinary?" Herbie echoed.

"And short. I can't even see the top shelf of my locker without standing on my tiptoes! Every time I think of asking Katrina to the party, I feel like a frog asking a princess to dance!"

Herbie stood up, his big toes just touching the handle bars. "A frog! That's a fine way to talk. You are, after all, God's creation—made in the image of God himself. I've never yet met a frog who could claim even a slight resemblance to his Maker!"

Andy wheeled his bike into the garage. He dismounted and stood there, looking at Herbie. "My mouth gets dry and my tongue goes numb every time I even say hello to her, Herbie. I know she won't go to the party with me. If only I were cuter or stronger or *taller!*"

"What you need, kid, is a good dose of self-confidence. Think of all the things you do well—from soccer to chess to chorus. Concentrate on your good points—your honesty, your sense of humor. Even your smile's not bad, considering you're stuck with *white* teeth," Herbie said, flashing a gold grin. "And remember, the most important thing is who you are inside."

Andy tucked his books under his arm. "But Katrina can't see the *inside* of me. All she sees is this redhaired, freckled dwarf!" Andy paused, then looked up at Herbie. "Can guardian angels tell the future?"

"Why?"

"Well, if I knew whether she'd say yes ..."

Herbie flew over to a carton of empty pop bottles. He sat cross-legged on top of one of the bottles and peered into another one. "Ah, I see something," he said, waving his hand, like a fortune teller, over the top of the pop bottle. "My crystal ball is in the dishwasher, but I can see almost as well in this dirty bottle."

Andy smiled. "And what do you see?"

Herbie bent over the tiny top of the bottle. "I see big paper flowers and chocolate cake."

"You sure it isn't white cake?" Andy asked.

"Oh, right. I mean white cake. And I see human beings laughing."

"Anyone I know?"

"Now that you ask," Herbie said, "one couple does look familiar. The girl's a knockout."

"What about the boy?"

"I can't make out his face. But he seems to be having a great time." Herbie straightened up. "Ah, the picture is fading, fading . . ."

"Tell me," Andy said, "was this lovely girl's date short?"

"It was hard to tell. People look taller when they feel good about themselves, when they don't think of themselves as frogs or dwarfs. But I did notice his date was wearing shoes with really low heels."

"All right already," Andy laughed. "I'll go call Katrina and ask her to the party."

"Because I have filled you with self-confidence?" Herbie asked.

"No," said Andy, grinning, "Because I sound taller on the phone."

* * *

For you created my inmost being; you knit me together in my mother's womb. I praise you because I am fearfully and wonderfully made.

(Psalm 139:13–14)

Angel In My Locker

Day 14

When he saw those boys from the high school leaning against the chain-link fence, Andy looked down and walked faster. He had seen the three of them there before, lots of times. But always before they had let him pass unnoticed.

Then he saw one of them move toward him, and he knew today was going to be different.

The tallest one stepped in front of Andy, blocking the sidewalk. Andy tried to go around him, but every time Andy swerved sideways, so did the boy.

"Hey, buddy, what's your hurry?" the boy said, placing his arm around Andy's shoulders. "Me and my business associates here want to have a little talk with you. Won't you step into our office?" He smiled a crooked smile as he took Andy's arm and forced him toward the fence. The other guys laughed. Andy looked around frantically, but in his hurry to get home from school he had outdistanced all the other students. Even Herbie was nowhere in sight.

"Here, sport. Have a joint—no charge!" The big one

stuck a lumpy little cigarette with twisted ends into Andy's shirt pocket. Then he smiled that crooked smile. "This is high-quality grass. A little of this and the whole stinkin' world looks good."

The third guy snickered. "Relax, punk. We just want to be your friends. Smoke that joint tonight and you'll see. It smooths out the wrinkles in your life." He smacked Andy playfully on the cheek. "It's time you grew up."

The tall one let go of his arm. Andy's heart seemed to pound like bass drums in his ears, but still he could hear their laughter as he ran toward home.

He stopped in front of the big trash can in the park. In red letters it said DO NOT LITTER. He pushed open its metal mouth and dropped the joint into it.

"Good place for it, kid." Herbie appeared, hovering above the trash can.

"*Now* you show up! Where were you when I needed you?" Still shaking, Andy sat down on one of the nearby picnic tables.

Angel In My Locker

"Close by—same as always. But you weren't in any danger. The three stooges were just looking for new customers."

Andy picked up a pine cone and began pulling it apart. "I know those guys are jerks. But I've been wondering about this whole drug thing. My friend Gene says his big brother smokes joints and that they smell sweet, like caramel corn. I know lots of people who smoke cigarettes and drink alcohol. Even some of my teachers." Andy looked up at Herbie. "If marijuana isn't any worse than those, would a little be so bad?" They headed toward the empty playground.

"And that guy said marijuana 'smooths out the wrinkles' in life. My life seems to have a *lot* of wrinkles lately."

Andy sank into the black rubber swing. Herbie took the one next to him.

"Use your head, kid. Dope—*any* kind—is for dopes. It doesn't solve anybody's problems. And when the high is gone, users find themselves with a few *more* problems—like dependency and an expensive drug habit. Besides, escaping from your troubles isn't the answer."

"So what is, then?" Andy asked.

"Learning from problems, growing past problems, living through problems—that's the answer.

"You see, kid, your body is not just a mass of cells and tissue and protoplasm, like you learned in biology. It's something much more. It's the temple of the Holy Spirit, and God has given you the job of keeping that temple clean and healthy."

"But what about everybody else? They do whatever they *want* to their 'temples.'"

"Remember the poster hanging in the guidance office at school?" Herbie asked.

"The one in fancy black letters?"

Herbie nodded. "That's the one. It's a quotation from Thoreau, one of the greatest thinkers of the nineteenth century. 'If a man does not keep pace with his companions, perhaps it is because he hears a different drummer. Let him step to the music which he hears, however measured or far away.'

"Sometimes you may feel 'out of step.' It may seem like *everybody's* taking drugs or smoking cigs or drinking booze. And the easy thing will be for you to become like them. But don't do it, kid. The drummer you must listen to is not the drummer of the world, calling you to mess up your life like everybody else. Instead, listen in your heart for the beat of the Holy Spirit, calling you to a life of fullness and joy in the Lord.

"And one more thing. You don't have to jump off a cliff to know that it's a long way down. And you don't have to experiment with sin to know that it *is* sin. Now—ready to go home?"

"Not quite," Andy said. "First I want to get high. Real high." He leaned back in the swing and began to pump his legs back and forth. Soon he was flying through the air, his feet reaching for the sky. "Think this is high enough, Herbie?" he laughed.

And feeling the swoosh of cool air on his face, the racing of his heart as he pumped his way into sky blue space, Andy knew this had to be the best high of all.

* * *

Do you not know that your body is a temple of the Holy Spirit, who is in you, whom you have received from God? You are not your own; you were bought at a price. Therefore honor God with your body.

(1 Corinthians 6:19–20)

Day 15

*W*hat a super day it's been, God! Andy looked out his window at the night sky. Tiny points of light poked through the blackness, and Andy tried to find some of the stars he had learned about at the planetarium that day.

Boy, God, it was a great field trip, Andy prayed. *On the way back we stopped at McDonald's, and Scarlet Daye—this really truly beautiful girl in my class—let me buy her a chocolate shake. So I sat with her the rest of the way to school, our shoulders touching all the way there.*

And the planetarium was excellent!

I've never thought much about stars, God. For me they're just one of those things that's always been around, like clouds or trees or my big cousin Josh. But when I settled into that thick chair, and that dark dome burst into stars—wow! What a sight!

And then as the planetarium man talked, tiny arrows of light pointed out constellations, the North Star, all sorts of neat stuff. Then he told how sailors and other people have been using the stars as a map for thousands of years. And I remembered my history teacher telling how Harriet Tubman always guided runaway slaves by using the North Star. And I remembered the story of the wise men, following that special bright star to the exact place where you were.

So tonight, God, I want to thank you—for chocolate milk shakes, for field trips, and for stars. Especially for stars.

"Quite a light show tonight," Herbie said as he landed on the window ledge.

"That's for sure," Andy said. "When God decides to create something, he really does excellent work."

Herbie smiled his gold smile. "Know what I like best about stars?"

"What?"

"Even though there are so many of them, each one is different. They weren't punched out with a giant cookie cutter, identical replicas of each other. God created each with its own splendor and then spangled them against the night sky."

Angel In My Locker

"You mean no two stars are alike?" Andy asked.

Herbie replied, "No more than any two people are. Each human being is a unique combination, a special creation. God doesn't want cookie-cutter people any more than he wanted cookie-cutter stars."

"I guess it would get boring if we all looked like gingerbread men and acted like robots," Andy said as he stretched out in bed.

"There's something else you should know about stars."

"What's that?" Andy snuggled down beneath his covers and closed his eyes.

"God's greatest creation is not the constellations, not the spinning planets, not the twinkling millions that brighten the night. God's greatest creation is *you*."

Andy opened his eyes and looked at Herbie. "Really, Herbie?"

"Really, kid. And as you yourself said—God *does do excellent work!*"

* * *

Lift your eyes and look to the heavens: Who created all these? He who brings out the starry host one by one, and calls them each by name. Because of his great power and mighty strength, not one of them is missing.

(Isaiah 40:26)

Day 16

Andy half lifted, half dragged the battered garbage can to the curb. He went back to the garage for the other one. He looked at the stack of full trash bags. His mom had finally finished cleaning out the attic; his dad had organized the basement. And both had piled the unwanted trash in the garage. Andy's job was to carry it to the curb so the garbage trucks could pick it up in the morning.

Herbie sat on the top trash bag, poking his big toe at the tiny white tie that held it closed. "So how's it going, kid?"

"Terrible. I'm so tired of grown-ups telling me what to do! It's always the same things." Andy's voice took on a sing-songy, sarcastic tone. "They say, 'Eat your peas,' and 'Practice your clarinet,' and 'Run two more laps.' Or they tell you to 'Rewrite your essay in ink,' or 'Turn off the TV,' or 'Be home before dark.'" Andy kicked at a nearby bag. "But their favorite is 'Take out the trash!'"

"So you think you're getting a raw deal?" Herbie asked, flying down and standing on the hood of the family Oldsmobile.

Angel In My Locker

"You bet!" Andy yelled. "You'd think I was some kind of baby, the way they all order me around. Mom, Dad, the coach, my teachers—everybody runs my life. Everybody except me. And I'm sick of it, Herbie! What's the use of having good sense if nobody lets me use it?" Andy picked up a big bag of trash and threw it over his shoulder, Santa Claus style. "Grown-ups have it made."

Andy trudged down the driveway, dropped the bag near the garbage cans, and came back for more.

Herbie met him at the garage door. "Remember last Saturday when your father worked overtime?"

"Yeah, sure. I remember. So what?" Andy grabbed another trash bag.

"He'd much rather have played golf or watched baseball or gone to the beach."

"So why didn't he?"

"He knew your family needed the extra money he'd make from working."

Andy made another trip down the driveway. Herbie waited for him in the garage.

"You know," Herbie said, "your mother missed having lunch with a group of her friends to bake those cookies for your Boy Scout troop."

Without a word Andy grabbed another bag of trash and started for the curb.

When he returned, Herbie said, "Your coach seemed kind of gruff at last night's practice, didn't he?" Andy stopped for a minute and nodded his head. "He had a 102-degree temperature and could hardly breathe, but he knew he had to be at practice."

Andy dragged another bag down the driveway. As he started back to the garage, Herbie met him halfway. "Take a break, kid," Herbie said as he settled on one of the low branches in the red maple. Andy plopped down in the grass near its trunk.

"Do you remember," Herbie asked, "when you and your cousin went to the state fair last summer?"

"Sure. We had a great time! I've never seen so many rides and games." Andy smiled. "Josh even won this huge purple unicorn."

"You went through the House of Mirrors, didn't you?"

"What a trip!" Andy laughed. "Some made you short and fat; others made you tall and skeleton-skinny. And some gave you huge heads and dwarfish bodies."

"It was funny and silly—and unreal," Herbie said. "The point is this, kid: Things aren't always what they appear to be."

Andy looked up at Herbie. "Meaning?"

"Being grown up isn't all it seems. It looks like fun—getting to be the boss. And it looks like freedom—getting to be in charge. But it's mostly hard work and responsibility."

"Hard work and responsibility!" Andy echoed, getting up and heading for the garage. "In that case," he said, grabbing two trash bags and starting down the drive, "I'll just think of this as basic training. With all this 'hard work and responsibility' experience, I'm going to make one great adult!"

Andy lined all the bags in neat rows near the curb.

"You know, kid," Herbie said, still sitting on the tree limb, "I won't be a bit surprised if you do." And through the clusters of red leaves, Andy could see the golden glint of Herbie's smile.

* * *

Listen to advice and accept instruction,
and in the end you will be wise.
(Proverbs 19:20)

Angel In My Locker 77

Day 17

Andy scanned the opened newspapers spread out all over his bedroom floor, looking for articles about South America. Before Friday, he had to find twenty. Then he would mount them and put them in his social studies notebook.

As he read the papers, he realized for the first time how much news was *bad* news. FIRE TAKES LIVES OF FOUR CHILDREN. BODY OF MISSING WOMAN FOUND. HURRICANE DESTROYS CITY.

The bad news headlines bothered Andy. But there was something else that had been bothering him, too.

There's this kid at school, God, Andy prayed. *His name is Robbie, and his legs are all bent and twisted. He has these special crutches, and you can hear him coming down the hall: clomp-thump, clomp-thump.*

When I went uptown to the museum last week, I saw a blind man walking down the street. He felt along in front of him with a cane. I could hear its tap, tap, tap above the sound of traffic.

Even now, while I'm praying, tons of bad things are happening all over the world.

I've been thinking about this a lot, God. And it just isn't right. It's just not fair.

Andy heard the rustling of newspaper and opened his eyes. Herbie scuffed his way through the papers, pausing here and there to read a headline. "I tell you, kid," Herbie said, "whoever said 'no news is good news' must have been talking about the newspaper business."

Andy put down his scissors and stretched out on the floor. "Aren't the headlines awful, Herbie?"

"Gruesome."

"When I was a little kid in Sunday school, I learned the verse 'God is love.'"

"First John four eight," Herbie said.

"But now I'm beginning to wonder. Does God love some people less than others? Is that why he lets them be crippled or blind or sick? And what about all the robbery and murder and war in the world? Why do all these things happen if God's the one in charge?"

Angel In My Locker

Herbie shuddered, and for just an instant Andy thought he saw his wings droop. "The problem of evil in the world," Herbie said. "Even we angels have trouble understanding it."

Then Herbie stretched out his wings and flew up on the bed. Andy got up and sat beside him.

"It really all goes back to the Garden of Eden," Herbie began, "when Adam and Eve chose to eat of the tree of the knowledge of good and evil. You see, God created man to be a free moral agent."

"A free loyal what?" Andy asked.

"Not *loyal*," Herbie smiled. "I said *moral*—a free moral agent. In other words, man is free to choose the way of light and life. But he is also free to choose the way of darkness and death. Many of the evils in this world—murder, deceit, cruelty, rebellion—are the direct result of evil choices by individuals, leaders, even nations who turn their backs on God."

"But that doesn't explain my friend Robbie. Or the blind man I saw uptown."

"No, it doesn't, kid. Neither of them has done anything to deserve his handicap. And you must realize that Robbie's crippled legs and the old man's blind eyes are not sent from God. They're just part of life in this imperfect, sin-filled world. The Bible tells us that there'll always be wars, poverty, hunger, unhappiness, death." Herbie paused for a moment, as a sad look came into his eyes. "And bad things will often happen to good people."

"Why does God *let* it happen?" Andy asked.

Herbie brightened. "God doesn't promise you a life free from problems. What he *does* promise you is that he'll be with you through every trouble, that he'll help you with every problem."

"Sometimes I think, 'That's just not fair!' Do you mean sometimes it's really *not* fair?"

"That's right, kid. It's all part of being human, of being born into a sinful world."

Andy looked at the harsh black headlines scattered across his floor. "Will it ever get better, Herbie?"

Why does God let bad things happen?

"Maybe not down here," Herbie said. "But there *is* a perfect place, one with no death or pain or tears or sadness. I call it home."

Andy smiled. "But we call it heaven, right?"

"Right. God is getting it ready for all the people who love him, who choose his way. No evil can ever enter there—and no one will need crutches or white-tipped canes."

"Tell me, Herbie, is heaven *really* neat?"

"Are you kidding?" Herbie flew up in the air and began waving his arms like a politician making a speech. "The gates are solid pearl! The walls are filled with emeralds and sapphires and lots of other jewels. The angel choirs sing all the time. God himself lights the whole place with a brightness like ten thousand suns. The streets are even shinier gold than my teeth! And . . ."

Herbie stopped talking and hovered above Andy's bed. After a few seconds he said, "Come on. Let's finish finding articles so we can clean up this mess."

"But aren't you going to tell me any more about the gates of pearl and the streets of gold?"

"Not now, kid. All this talk of heaven is making me homesick!"

* * *

Hate what is evil; cling to what is good. . . . Do not be overcome by evil, but overcome evil with good.
(Romans 12:9, 21)

Angel In My Locker   81

Day 18

The chugging weight of the passing freight train made the pavement beneath Andy's tennis shoes quiver. The air was filled with the hum of steel against steel, till the caboose finally disappeared down the track. Andy stood next to the rails, looking down the rows of ties that narrowed and narrowed and finally melted into the horizon.

Herbie fluttered into view. "Those trains are certainly *noisy* creatures!"

"I like the sound. It sounds like energy and adventure." Andy picked up a handful of rocks from between the rails and began throwing them down the track. "You know, Herbie, I've spent my whole life watching trains pass me by. Huge freight trains—boxcars full of fruit and flatcars loaded with steel. Red cabooses. Passenger trains. The faces at their windows are blurred by the speed.

"But they all leave me standing here, wondering where they're going. Sometimes I want to just hop on one of those trains and feel myself hurled forward to somewhere."

Where?" Herbie asked.

"*Anywhere!*" Andy yelled. "I'm tired of the same sidewalks, the same street corners, the same houses the same people. I'm just so *totally* bored, Herbie! There's nothing to do around here."

Andy crossed the tracks and walked toward home. Herbie settled lightly on his shoulder.

"What is it with you human beings? You all seem to suffer from 'itchy foot.' Everyone wants to explore the unknown, to travel to new places. When he was on earth, even Jesus did."

I'm just so totally bored, Herbie!
There's nothing to do around here.

"Jesus felt this way, too?" Andy asked. "Don't tell me they had freight trains in Nazareth."

"Almost," Herbie grinned. "Jesus was just about your age when he realized how small his hometown of

Nazareth was. He used to watch as caravans—carrying spices and silks and dark-eyed women—criss-crossed the desert. Their camels would cast long, inviting shadows across the sand. And Jesus wanted to follow them—to know something other than the smell of freshly cut lumber and the feel of rough timbers in Joseph's carpenter shop."

"And did he? Did he go with one of the caravans?"

Herbie shook his head. "Never. During his whole lifetime on earth, Jesus' travels never took him further than two hundred miles from Nazareth."

"That's not so far. Aunt Libby's is farther than that."

"And yet," Herbie continued, "no world traveler has ever accomplished as much as Jesus did. No businessman who jets daily to exotic, faraway cities ever conducted business as important as his."

"I know," Andy said, turning down the front sidewalk to his house. "But I'm still bored."

"You've got some growing to do, kid. And sometimes your mind and your imagination will grow faster than your surroundings do. So the big temptation will be to say how *totally* bored you are. But you don't have to be."

"What am I supposed to do," Andy asked, "hop a freight?"

"Not quite. Look for new experiences where you are: a hobby, a game, a club, a good book, a kind deed, a new friend. You get the idea."

The distant sound of a passing train rippled through the air. "Will I ever get to go anywhere exciting, Herbie?"

"You may be surprised where those trains eventually take you. Could be New York or Los Angeles or Chicago or Tampa."

"Sounds good to me!" Andy smiled. "When do I leave?"

"Not for quite a while. But until then, remember this: *Circumstances* are not boring. Only *people* have the capacity to be boring." Herbie paused and smiled. "And the choice is *totally* yours!"

* * *

And the child [Jesus] grew and became strong; he was filled with wisdom, and the grace of God was upon him.
(Luke 2:40)

Day 19

Andy stood on the front porch of Engel's Funeral Home. Even out here he could hear the whiny sounds of organ music. He closed his eyes and tried to take a deep breath of fresh air. But his chest hurt and his throat felt as if it were full of unswallowed liver.

Grandpa died yesterday, God. Andy squeezed his eyes tighter shut and kept praying. *We drove all night to get here for the funeral. Mom hasn't stopped crying, and Dad just stands around looking real sad—and older, somehow.*

Grandpa lies in a casket lined with gray satin, his hands folded across his stomach. He looks asleep— sort of. I don't like to look at him, God. I keep thinking he'll open his eyes, laugh that deep laugh of his, and ask me how my curve ball's coming.

But deep down inside, I know he won't—ever.

There are flowers everywhere: pink ones and red ones and even orange ones. The air is heavy with their smell. It makes my head ache and my eyes water. Or maybe these are tears. I hope I'm not too old to cry.

It's all real sad, God. Grandpa wasn't so very old, and he was hardly ever sick. Why did he have to die? He was such a good guy; I really loved him.

"Hey, kid. How's it going?" Herbie stood on the porch railing, looking up at Andy.

Andy shrugged his shoulders. "Not so good."

"Yeah, I know." From inside came the sound of someone crying. "Have time for a walk around the parking lot?"

"Sure. Why not?"

Andy came down the big front steps and began to walk toward the edge of the lot. Herbie flew after him and perched on his shoulder. For a few moments, neither of them spoke.

Then Herbie said, "Remember in elementary school how every spring you would plant a bean in a milk carton?"

Andy nodded. "We'd line them up in the window

Angel In My Locker

where we could watch them all day while we did our school work."

"And after you planted the bean, it would just lie there underneath the dirt—quiet and invisible and dead, or so it seemed."

"I was always scared that my bean wouldn't grow. I was afraid all the other kids would have a plant and I would just have a milk carton of muddy dirt," Andy said.

"But it never happened that way," Herbie said. "And one sunny morning, as you all crowded around, someone would notice a tiny green shoot sticking shyly up from the black soil. And then the room would be full of squeals and cheers and clapping."

"I remember," Andy smiled. "It looked different from the bean we planted, and yet it was the same."

"That's the way it is with your grandpa, kid. His old body lies there in the funeral home, stiff and dead. But his soul—that part of him that thinks and feels and loves— is alive! And it will always be alive, because your grandpa has taken the only road there is to eternal life—death."

Andy stopped at the porch steps. "But I miss him, Herbie. I miss him lots! I—" Andy's voice shook and then seemed lost somewhere inside him.

As Andy crossed the porch and started inside, he felt a tugging in his back pocket. He reached his hand around just as Herbie pulled out the big white handkerchief. "Here, kid, use this," Herbie said. "Because you're *never* too old to cry."

*   *   *

I am the resurrection and the life. He who believes in me will live, even though he dies.

(John 11:25)

Angel In My Locker

Day 20

Andy dumped out the contents of the coffee can. Crumpled dollar bills and piles of coins scattered across the top of his dresser. He began organizing them into stacks, counting as he went along. Every time Andy uncrumpled a bill and laid it on the pile, Herbie would snatch it, fold it into a paper airplane, and send it sailing across the room.

"Cut it out, Herbie!" Andy growled.

Herbie sat on top of his latest creation and glided around the room. "Pilot to control tower. Pilot to control tower. Request permission to land." He swooped down toward the dresser and brought the dollar-bill airplane to a halt near the stack of quarters. "Hey, kid, where'd you get all the money?"

Andy held the coffee can over the edge of the dresser and began raking the money back into it. "I saved it—a few lousy bits at a time. But I might as well stop trying. I'll *never* have enough to buy the things I want!" He snapped the lid on the can.

Angel In My Locker

"So what kinds of things do you want to save up for?" Herbie asked.

"All kinds of things—like a minibike, a stereo with four-foot speakers, a new Shakespeare rod, a fiberglass sailboat, a go-cart. I could go on and on, but what's the use? I'm lucky to have popcorn-and-movies money. Mom and Dad plead 'hard times' whenever I ask for anything. And if relatives send a little cash my way, for my birthday or Christmas, Mom stashes it in the bank for my college fund."

"Well," Herbie said, "college is important—"

Andy cut him off. "I'm sick of being broke! I'm tired of being poor, of mowing lawns and delivering papers just to make pocket money." Andy began drawing dollar signs all over a piece of art paper. "I want to be rich, Herbie! Not just 'well off,' but *rich*. Poverty has zero appeal for me."

Herbie pulled Andy's Bible off the bookshelf and pushed it across the desk toward him.

Andy watched him. "Any get-rich quick schemes in there?"

Herbie ignored the question and opened the Bible to Matthew. "Read this, kid. Chapter six, verse twenty-one."

Andy took the Bible and read, " 'For where your treasure is, there your heart will be also.' " He looked up at Herbie. "So what's that mean? I have to take a vow of poverty or something?"

"Listen," Herbie said, placing one hand on his hip and pointing at Andy with the other, "this is important. In his parables Jesus warned again and again how hard it is for a rich man to enter the kingdom of heaven— not because God doesn't like rich people and not because he expects all Christians to live on poverty row. The reason is the one you read. 'Where your treasure is, there your heart will be also.' If you become obsessed with material things, you soon forget about God. And money gives people a false sense of power. Wealthy people often feel they don't need God, that they—and their money—can handle any situation."

"I didn't realize that wanting nice things could lead to sin," Andy said.

"It's only natural for you to want the things money can buy," Herbie went on. "But be careful. Remember the story of King Midas?"

"Sure," Andy laughed. "Everything he touched turned to gold—even his food. Pretty soon he was willing to trade all his gold for a turkey drumstick."

"Right. And the moral of Midas is as important as it is obvious: Some things are more important than money. In fact, money can't buy the most important things."

"Like good health," Andy said, remembering his pneumonia. "And my friends and family."

"Even salvation comes as a gift," Herbie said.

Andy tore out the piece of art paper he had been drawing on and wadded it up. Then he smiled. "Does this mean I can never be a millionaire?"

"Just don't be too quick to snub your nose at the poor folk in this world. Once a simple preacher—with no home, no possessions, no money—changed the course of the world."

Andy looked at Herbie for a few seconds. "Jesus?" he asked.

"Bingo, kid!" Herbie said, grabbing the wadded-up paper and spiking it, volleyball style, across the room and into Andy's wastebasket.

* * *

Keep your lives free from the love of money and be content with what you have, because God has said, "Never will I leave you; never will I forsake you."

(Hebrews 13:5)

Angel In My Locker

Day 21

*I*f people died of embarrass-
ment, God, I'd be laid out cold somewhere right now!

Andy threw down his glove and baseball cap and
slammed his bedroom door.

*How could Dad do that to me, God? I told him it
was no big deal if he missed my Little League games.
I knew he had to scrape and paint the trim on the
windows and clean out the gutters, and do some
other stuff Mom had written on a list. But I guess he
didn't believe me.*

Andy got out a pair of shorts and a T-shirt and
began unsnapping his baseball shirt.

*I was having a great game, God. It was the bot-
tom of the sixth, and we were ahead three-zip when
Dad showed up. I was on the pitcher's mound, burn-
ing them past the batters. Until I saw him.*

*Dad was wearing this old plaid shirt with a
ripped pocket. His gray work pants were all splotched
with white paint, and he actually had them tucked
inside his scuffed-up combat boots! He was even*

wearing that old fishing hat Mom keeps trying to throw away.

I could have died, God. I looked around to see whether any of the guys had noticed. They were all still chattering away, but I knew they had seen him. He stuck out like a green elephant in a snow storm!

I tried to get my concentration back, but it was gone. My pitches got worse and worse. And Dad kept yelling, "Come on, Son! That's my boy!" Then everybody knew we were related. It was awful, God! I felt my ears turning red. The next three batters got hits off me. Then the coach pulled me out of the game.

Andy threw his cleats into the bottom of his closet.

I didn't say much on the way home. Dad thought it was because we lost, and he kept talking about sportsmanship and "it's how you play the game that counts" and other stuff I've heard about a million times before. He even wanted to stop at the Dairy Queen and buy me a shake, but I told him my stomach hurt. I really just didn't want to be seen with him."

Angel In My Locker

Andy scooped up his dirty uniform and started down the hallway toward the clothes hamper. He met Herbie coming out of the bathroom, his tiny gold toothbrush in his hand.

"How can parents be so stupid, Herbie?" Andy asked. "Sometimes I think they deliberately do things to embarrass me. And I hate it!" He shoved his uniform deep into the hamper.

Do you think he deliberately wanted to embarrass you?

"You must mean the 'unforgivable' thing your father did at the baseball game," Herbie said.

"You bet. Unforgivable is the right word."

"Imagine," Herbie said, "a father so anxious to get to his son's game that he didn't take time to change clothes. Imagine a father so proud of his boy, so eager to see him play that he rushed to the game the minute he finished his chores, work clothes and all. Doesn't that sound 'unforgivable' to you?"

Andy looked surprised, then confused. He stared down at his bare toes a long time before he said, "I got some homework to do. See you later, Herbie."

After dinner that night Andy stretched out on his bed and began organizing his baseball cards. Herbie sat on the pillow, examining the bristles in his toothbrush.

"Tell me the truth, Herbie," Andy began. "Did Dad really show up at the ball diamond dressed weird just because he was so anxious to see me play?"

"Use your head, kid," Herbie said, tapping Andy's temple with his gold toothbrush. "Do you think he deliberately wanted to embarrass you?"

"No, I guess not," Andy said slowly.

"Remember last month at the family reunion when you and your cousins were playing hide-and-seek?" Herbie asked.

Andy blushed. "How could I forget it! I ended up face-down in a mud puddle behind the barn."

"You weren't exactly the picture of neatness, your hair hanging in dripping strands and your clothes spattered with smelly mud."

"That's for sure!"

"But your father was the first one to show up at your side, and he wrapped his own shirt around your shoulders."

Andy fingered the edge of a Hank Aaron card. "But he *really* embarrassed me, Herbie!"

Andy could feel Herbie looking at him. "Listen, kid. Don't wallow in self-pity; it's even worse than barnyard mud."

Andy gathered up the scattered baseball cards. "Maybe you're right."

"*Maybe* I'm right?" Herbie grinned.

"Okay, okay," Andy laughed. "You *are* right. But I still think Dad's combat boots and fishing hat stink!"

"I know what you mean, kid. I feel the same way about barnyard mud."

* * *

Each of you should look not only to your own interests, but also to the interests of others.

(Philippians 2:4)

Day 22

Dad pulled up in front of the Deerwood Nursing Home. Andy peered out the back window. What a creepy looking place! It reminded him of some haunted house on the late, late show. He began to wish he'd stayed home with Megan and the baby-sitter.

They parked near the wide porch lined with high-backed rockers and went in. Andy's nose burned. The whole place smelled the way the bathroom did whenever Mom used disinfectant. As they walked down the hall, they passed many people sitting against the wall in wheel chairs. Everyone was so *old!* Their faces seemed to be solid wrinkles.

Andy's mom stopped near an open door at the end of the hallway. For a moment she stood there, her hand against the white door frame. Then she smiled a smile that Andy knew was fake and went in. Dad and Andy followed.

Aunt Ida was sitting in a big orange chair with a tray attached. A folded sheet was tied around her middle and held her upright in the chair. Her mouth didn't close quite right, and spit kept dripping out of the side. They had a huge bib fastened around her neck.

"Aunt Ida." Mom said loudly, "you're looking so good! Did you get over that cold of yours? Everybody feels better once spring comes." Mom kept talking, a mile a minute. Andy could tell she was nervous.

Andy looked closely at Aunt Ida. Her eyes reminded him of gray marbles. She stared, unblinking, at the wall. Andy wondered if Aunt Ida even heard what his mother was saying.

Then they brought her lunch tray—some slimy brown stuff that looked like burned oatmeal. Just the smell of it made Andy want to gag.

"Tell Aunt Ida about your baseball team, Andy," Mom said. She smiled that fake smile and said through her teeth, "Go on. Talk to her."

Andy started to open his mouth—and then clamped it shut. The disinfectant and the slimy oatmeal and Aunt Ida as a zombie were all too much for him. Without looking at his parents he ran out of the room. He didn't stop running until he was inside his own car. He leaned his forehead against the window and saw his own reflection look back at him.

"Hey, kid."

Andy turned and saw Herbie straddling the gearshift, his bare legs and feet hanging down from under his robe.

"Oh, Herbie, it was awful!"

"Tell me about it."

Aunt Ida's eyes reminded him of gray marbles.

"Aunt Ida isn't anything like I remember her. And Mom kept trying to get me to talk about baseball. Then they brought this mushy stuff for her lunch. I felt like I was going to throw up or—worse yet—cry!" Andy looked out the window. "Aunt Ida used to make fried chicken whenever we'd visit. And she could bake the biggest, fluffiest biscuits!" He looked back at Herbie, who was now standing on the dashboard. "Why does getting old have to be so awful, Herbie?"

"It doesn't always have to be. Remember Mr. Kelly down the street?"

"Sure. He's the one who always dresses up like a hunchback to hand out his Halloween candy."

"Well, he's old. And you know Mrs. Osborn who makes that special nut fudge every Christmas?"

Andy nodded.

"She's old, too. Moses was eighty when he went back to Egypt to lead the children of Israel out. And Noah was six hundred years old when he went into the ark!"

"But what about Aunt Ida?"

"Aunt Ida, like most of the other people you saw in the nursing home, has health problems. Her famous fried chicken wouldn't do her much good now, since she has no teeth. She needs lots of special care, the kind the doctors and nurses here can provide for her. But her biggest problem is one shared by all older people—sick or healthy."

"What's that?"

"Loneliness. Everyone is in such a hurry. No one has time to talk—or listen—to the elderly. And they have so much to share! When you get home, why not visit with Mrs. Wise for a few minutes when you deliver her paper? She's always sitting in the porch swing, waiting. Did you know Mr. Kelly has a huge model train set up in his basement? And maybe Aunt Ida *would* like to hear about your baseball team."

Andy took a deep breath and pushed open the car door. As he walked across the nursing home lawn, he bent down and picked a bright, fuzzy dandelion. He remembered how, when he was little, he used to take Aunt Ida dandelion bouquets, and she would put them in a blue vase on the coffee table.

Andy walked into the room and straight over to Aunt Ida. He laid the yellow flower in her hand and, pulling his chair close to hers, began, "Let me tell you all about my baseball team, Aunt Ida. . . ."

* * *

This is my command: Love each other.

(John 15:17)

Angel In My Locker   101

Day 23

$\mathbb{A}$ndy leaned against the garage. All day long its boards had been soaking up the sun, and now he could feel their warmth through his jersey. He closed his eyes and began his prayer.

My friend Tommy has a problem, God—and I figure you're just the one to solve it for him. You see, Tommy's parents just got divorced.

He lives with his mom in an apartment on Wabash Street. His dad lives about two hours away, and Tommy only gets to see him on long weekends and holidays. Before the divorce, Tommy and his folks lived out in the country. Tommy had a dog, two cats, and a rabbit. But now he can't even have a gerbil. His landlord thinks all animals stink.

He says his mother cries a lot, too. When his dad comes to pick him up, his parents almost always end up yelling at each other. And it makes Tommy feel rotten.

Tommy's parents have ruined his whole life with this stupid divorce, God. Can't you get his mom and

*dad back together again so everything will be like it
was before* ?

Andy opened his eyes. The sun had begun to set,
and the yard was taking on a blue, twilight look. A slight
tremor in the snowball bush sent tiny, star-shaped petals
to the ground. Herbie emerged from among the white
blossoms.

"I didn't even see you in there," Andy said.

Herbie smiled and touched his robe. "This is the
perfect camouflage outfit for snowball bushes."

Andy sat down in the grass by the back fence.
Herbie settled himself in a cluster of clover.

"Why do people get divorced, Herbie?" Andy asked.

"Oh, lots of different reasons. Sometimes they stop
loving each other. Sometimes one partner changes so
much that it's like being married to someone you hardly
know. And sometimes one or both people fall in love
with someone else. It isn't right, but it happens. And
then so does divorce. God's best plan for humans is
one marriage and two parents, but more and more often
that's not the way it works out."

Angel In My Locker

"I'm worried about my friend Tommy."

"Yeah, I know. Your friend Tommy has lots of problems to deal with—and so do his parents."

"His parents are the *cause* of all the problems. What problems do they have? Wasn't the divorce what they wanted?" Andy asked.

"Tommy's folks are confused and scared and unhappy. On top of everything else, they're feeling guilty. They both need Tommy's help, his acceptance, and his love." Herbie said.

"Will his folks ever like each other again?"

"In time they'll stop being angry with each other, but Tommy's folks will never again love each other and want to be together. That's what's known as reality, and both you and Tommy need to accept it."

"But can't God do something about it?"

"God, of course, can do anything. But he's not in the habit of zapping couples back together against their will. He doesn't cast people in rigid roles and keep them from making choices. Or mistakes. What he does do is to keep on loving people—even when they mess up."

"Tommy's folks have sure messed up! Our Sunday-school teacher calls divorced families 'broken homes.'"

Herbie nodded. "Things are always changing, kid. Nothing stays the same. Tommy's life will never be like it was before the divorce. But God has a marvelous way of putting pieces together."

"Even broken pieces?"

"*Especially* broken pieces," Herbie said. "You might want to tell your friend Tommy that."

Andy was quiet for a moment, chewing on a grass blade. "Maybe I will," he said. "Just maybe I will."

* * *

I am he who will sustain you. I have made you and I will carry you; I will sustain you and I will rescue you.

(Isaiah 46:4)

Angel In My Locker

Day 24

"Sometimes Mom makes me so mad!" The ball whizzed toward him, and Andy swung. A swoosh of air was the only sound.

"I think that's called a strike," Herbie called down. He hovered near the top of the batting cages.

"She treats me like a real baby!" Andy swung again, and the crack of his hit echoed across the grass. He tried to concentrate on the balls streaking toward him one at a time from the pitching machine. He tried to concentrate on his form. But he couldn't stop thinking about what his mother had said.

"Honest, Herbie, she treats me like I'm two years old. She tells me which shirt matches which pants. She insists on meeting all my friends. And she actually cried—in front of all the guys—when I wrecked my bike coming off the starting hill at last Saturday's BMX race!"

Andy had found his rhythm, and batted balls rolled far out into the netting. "But worst of all is how she nags me about things. 'Where are you going? Who else

Angel In My Locker

is going? When will you be back?' She makes me feel like a bug under a microscope! And now she won't let me go camping with the guys next Friday night." No more balls came, so he left the cage and stuck the Louisville Slugger into a big can with lots of other bats.

Andy walked across the street to the park and splashed his flushed face with water from the drinking fountain. He sat down on a nearby bench and stared through the chain-link fence at the empty tennis courts. "A baby, Herbie. She thinks I'm a baby."

Herbie appeared on the back of the bench and sat down on the top slat. "Is this camping trip a big deal?" he asked.

"You bet it is!" Andy said. "Five of us guys were going to bike to Mt. Baldy, sleep under the stars, and then hike the dunes the next day. We've all been camping plenty of times with our families, and Noah is even an Eagle Scout! But Mom says, "Five boys shouldn't be out alone—all night—in wild terrain." Andy punched his leg. "She makes it sound more like an African safari than a simple camping trip to a local state park."

Herbie studied Andy's face. "You know, kid, Jesus' earthly mother was a lot like yours."

Andy's eyes widened. "You've got to be kidding!"

"No, really. When Jesus was twelve, he finally went with his parents to Jerusalem to celebrate the Passover. It was a sixty-mile walk! But still some of the families brought along little children and aging relatives. The caravan went *so* slowly—too slowly for Jesus and his friends. So they would race ahead, climb the jagged hillsides, and splash each other with icy brook water.

"But Mary always worried. She wanted Jesus at least to be in sight of the caravan. And later, in Jerusalem, when he stayed behind to talk with the leaders of the Temple—his mother was frantic! When she and Joseph finally found Jesus, Mary cried—in front of everyone!"

"And how did Jesus finally convince her that he wasn't her baby boy any longer?" Andy asked.

A baby, Herbie! She thinks I'm a baby.

Herbie smiled. "What makes you think he ever did? Listen kid, the camp-out sounds like fun—but it can keep for another year. Mt. Baldy and those sand dunes have been there for generations. They're not going anywhere in the next twelve months. Besides, that'll give you time to show your mother just how grown-up you really are."

"And exactly how do I do that?"

"By the way you treat your little sister, by the way you do your chores around the house, by the way you think of how others feel and not just what *you* want to do."

Andy groaned. "Herbie, will Mom ever stop thinking of me as her baby?"

"Someday your mother will realize that you are a capable and independent man. But she'll never stop trying to protect you from failure or hurt. And she'll never stop thinking of you as her baby."

"Never! Why not?"

"Because," Herbie smiled, "the *best* mothers never do."

* * *

Near the cross of Jesus stood his mother.

(John 19:25)

DAY 25

Andy tried not to scratch his back, but his sunburn was really beginning to itch. He took his post cards from the top of his tackle box and began to wedge them into the frame of his mirror.

I had a great time at the lake this weekend, God—jumping the waves, tubing down to the pier, floating on my back, and watching the sea gulls soar. And I loved the sand! Castles, roads, mountains—no one thinks you're a baby if you play in the sand at the beach. Even grown-ups build with it! Speckled, endless stuff—I haven't had so much fun since I gave away my Play-doh. It was just super, God!

Andy noticed a slight movement just above him—and there was Herbie, sitting on top of the mirror, shaking the sleeves of his robe. Tiny speckles of sand tumbled onto the dresser. "Ah," he said, "souvenirs!"

Andy laughed. "Wasn't the lake great, Herbie? As far as I could see there was water—blue-green waves splashing and crashing, whitecaps racing for shore. Every morning I took an early walk along the beach and left deep, barefoot prints the lake gulped for breakfast."

"It certainly was beautiful. When it comes to creation, you must admit that God did a *very* good job!" Herbie said.

God knew about outer space long before NASA did.

"Tell me, Herbie," Andy said. "Did God know, even then, that there'd be kids and inner tubes?"

"Of course he did!" Herbie said, fluttering down to straighten the bottom post card and seating himself on top of Andy's tackle box. "You see, kid, God is omniscient."

"Wow! Now that's what Mrs. Miles would call a 'fifty-cent word.'"

"The idea behind it is big, too. It means 'all knowing.' From the beginning to the end of time, nothing is hidden from God. All man's inventions were already in the mind of God."

Angel In My Locker

"All of them?"

"Every single one, from the wheel to the microdot. God knew about outer space long before NASA did. And we angels have been flying for millenniums." Herbie didn't speak for a moment. "There's something else God knows, too."

"What's that?"

"He knows *your* future—but not like some fortune teller who looks at crinkled tea leaves or wrinkled palms or smudged crystal balls."

"Or dirty pop bottles?" Andy smiled.

"Or dirty pop bottles," Herbie grinned. "God has a plan for your life. And day by day it will unfold, like a flower in time-lapse photography—when you see a bud burst into a real flower.

"There's joy and laughter and tears and pain and work and love and lots of other things waiting for you, kid."

"And they're *all* a part of God's plan?" Andy asked.

"Every single one," Herbie said. "Just as much as sea gulls and sunshine and inner tubes."

* * *

The Lord will guide you always.
(Isaiah 58:11)

Epilog

"Wow, kid, what a mess!"
Herbie said, looking into Andy's open locker.

"That's for sure, and before school's out next week
our lockers have to pass inspection. Mrs. Brockopp said
she wanted this 'disaster' clean if it took all homeroom
period to do it."

Andy began going through piles of wrinkled papers
that cluttered the bottom of his locker. "Look, Herbie.
Here's that overdue library book Mrs. Kellstrom keeps
yelling about. Hey—here's that math assignment I
couldn't find when I had to take a zero!" Andy
smoothed out the paper and laid it aside. "I'll see if Mr.
Forbes'll still take it."

Herbie flew up to the top shelf. "Let's see what's up
here. Four broken pencils. A dissected ink pen. A half-
eaten bag of potato chips. What's this?" Herbie unfolded
a piece of pink paper. "A note from Katrina!"

"Hey, give me that!" Andy grinned, grabbing it.

"And here's *another* one—from Scarlet!"

Andy blushed and snatched at the note.

Angel In My Locker

Herbie laughed. "Andy the lady killer. At the beginning of the year you couldn't even *talk* to a girl without sweating."

"Guess I've changed."

Herbie flew down and sat on a stack of books beside Andy's locker. "You really *have* changed, kid—in lots of ways."

Andy picked up a stack of papers and began leafing through them. "What ways?" he asked.

Someday—soon—you won't need me anymore.

"Well, for one thing, you've grown physically. Your shoes are bigger and your jeans are longer. But you've grown spiritually, too. You've learned to have more faith in God, to come to him with *any* problem. You've learned that the Bible really has something to say to you—that it's not just a storybook. And—most important of all—you're becoming more aware of the Holy Spirit, that small voice inside you that helps you make decisions, that lets you know God's will."

Andy looked at Herbie. "Will you always be my guardian angel?"

A look that Andy had never seen before came across Herbie's face. "Someday—soon—you won't need me anymore."

"I'll *always* need you, Herbie!"

Herbie sighed. "No, you won't, kid. You'll outgrow me the way you did night lights and teddy bears."

Before Andy could answer, the 8:45 bell blared the end of homeroom. And suddenly the hall swarmed with laughing, shouting, pushing students. Andy grabbed his books, slammed his locker shut, and headed for first hour.

It was several days later when Andy burst into his room, yelling, "Herbie, Herbie! School's out! Can you believe it? Now I'm a seventh-grader—and I even have a decent report card. I actually got an A from Mr. Albert!" Andy waved his grade card over his head. "Herbie! Herbie?"

The room was quiet. Very quiet. Andy could almost hear Goldie blowing bubbles.

"Herbie?" Andy said again, softer this time.

Then Andy noticed his Bible lying in the middle of the bed. When he left for school this morning, it had been on the shelf. He walked over and picked it up. It fell open to Psalm 121. Verses 7 and 8 were underlined. Andy read, "The Lord will keep you from all harm he will watch over your life; the Lord will watch over your coming and going both now and forevermore."

Andy stared down at his open Bible. It was then he noticed what had caused the Bible to fall open to that particular passage. A tiny gold toothbrush.

"Good-by, Herbie," Andy whispered. "And thanks— for everything."

From somewhere far away came the tinkling of wind chimes, stirred by a summer breeze.

JF
Carney
(I)

11-13

Independence Public Library